THE NEW TEXAS
WILD GAME
COOKBOOK

THE NEW TEXAS WILD GAME COOKBOOK

A Tradition Grows

Judith & Richard Morehead

With Woodcut Illustrations by Barbara Mathews Whitehead

1985 ★ EAKIN PRESS ★ Austin

First Printing 1972
Revised Printing 1985

Copyright © 1985
By Judith and Richard Morehead

Published in the United States of America
By Eakin Press, P.O. Box 23066, Austin, Texas 78735

ISBN 0-89015-526-7

THIS BOOK IS DEDICATED to all lovers of the outdoors, wild game and good eating. Skills learned in the long-ago are being improved steadily in the twentieth century by trial-and-error and the application of new knowledge and equipment.

Our education came from such fine cooks of the past as Katy Walker and Doris Herring . . . from great friends and outdoorsmen as Claud Gilmer of Rocksprings, Tom Waddell of Eagle Lake, and Jay Vessels of Austin.

Family and friends served as our laboratory . . . *Thanks* . . .

CONTENTS

FOREWORD

The authors of this book were grown and married (to each other) before game cooking became a serious interest. The opportunity for hunting and eating game hardly existed on the northwest Texas plains except for an occasional meal of doves, quail or wild duck. The region now provides much better hunting than fifty years ago, as does much of Texas.

As newlywed residents of Central Texas, a whole new world of pleasure opened for game cooking, particularly venison from the growing abundance of deer which are thriving despite Texas's population growth.

We are indebted to William D. Wittliff, an Austinite of many talents, for publishing the original *Texas Wild Game Cookbook* at his Encino Press in 1972, and to Edwin Eakin of Austin's Eakin Press for allowing us to expand it in 1985.

Most recipes in this book were unpublished before the 1972 edition. Many others have been added since. Many are original. Some were contributed by new or old friends. A richly rewarding experience has been the eagerness of others to share their favorite game cooking recipes. Some were handed down through generations in a family without previously being recorded. Others resulted from latter-year discovery in Texas kitchens.

One learns continuously about hunting and game cooking,

which adds fascination. Every good cook improvises. We hope this will serve as a starter, for we believe the art of good game cooking is just beginning for most Americans including the chefs of gourmet restaurants.

The authors have loved the years of experience, collecting, discussion (sometimes heated) and rich "togetherness" behind this volume. We hope it will help others, particularly young people, in appreciation of wildlife, in conservation, and in the enjoyment of the expanding art of cooking linked by unwritten recipes with our heritage.

Judith and Richard Morehead

GOOD HUNTING
. . . GOOD EATING

Wild game hunting and cooking are among mankind's oldest skills, and both are expanding constantly even in our urban society.

Lacking weapons other than stones and clubs, early man ate insects and plants because most animals and birds were too elusive. Over the years hunting equipment has improved mightily, but bagging game is still an outdoor exercise often frustrating to the hunter.

Game cooking probably started by accident when early man discovered fire and accidentally dropped a bird onto hot coals or set a haunch of venison too near the flame. To his surprise, our ancestor found the cooked meat was tender and juicy.

Today, expert game cooking is no haphazard matter. In homes with hunters, and a growing number of gourmet restaurants with knowledgeable chefs, good cooks have found many creative ways to prepare delicious wild game dishes.

Even some game is less wild than its ancestors. Game ranching is becoming a flourishing industry, with imported "exotics" from all over the world being stocked by Texas ranchers who find hunters-for-pay a profitable supplement to raising domestic livestock.

The exotics are new varieties of antelope, deer, sheep, goats and birds from Africa, Asia, and other foreign lands. The meat from such imports can be sold commercially, and the game isn't subject to hunting laws governing native wild game.

Likewise, pen-raised quail, wild turkeys and pheasants can be killed and sold at any time, although such birds are usually less wild than those born naturally, even after they are released to roam free. These can challenge many hunters, however, especially those who go afield only once or twice a year.

Such commercial hunting is expensive, but it takes less time than the traditional methods. Even hunting for truly wild native birds and animals is becoming high-priced, as landowners learn the value of wildlife conservation and production. Unfortunately, few places are left where one can knock on a farmer's door and be invited to go hunting — free — on his land.

The State of Texas offers numerous public hunts on preserves managed by the Parks and Wildlife Department. These are strictly regulated and applications usually out-number the available places.

One reason for increased interest in harvesting and eating wild game is growing evidence the meat is more nutritious and less caloric, in general, than its domestic counterpart.

It is still against the law for restaurants in most places, including Texas, to sell any game unless imported or pen-raised. In New York, however, gourmet markets and chic restaurants cater to the appetites of weight-conscious customers by selling game. Commercial hunters years ago brought a prohibition on sales, after causing passenger pigeons to become extinct and slaughtering waterfowl needlessly.

Times have changed greatly. Major game animals are increasing all over the United States.

Texas has many more whitetailed deer than ever before, also wild turkeys. The big birds were in danger of disappearing as recently as the 1930s. Thousands of delicious pheasants are being harvested annually in the grainfields of the Texas Panhandle, where none grew half a century ago.

Much credit for this favorable development goes to landowners and others with a pocketbook interest in hunting. Two million Texas hunters spend an estimated six hundred million dollars a year on their sport. The income helps many farmers and ranchers avoid bankruptcy. Conservation makes the land more valuable. A farm or ranch with good hunting sells for much more than land lacking game.

If food faddists take to the woods and deplete the game supply in the name of human health, it may be hazardous to distribute too widely the information that wild game is lower in fat and calories and higher in protein than equal quantities of beef, pork or domestic fowl. When weight-loss fans learn also how tasty well-prepared game can be, the competition with traditional hunters could become fierce.

Persons with access to good game eating long have praised its eating qualities. The uninitiated may still turn up their noses, but they don't know what they're missing. It is so much more than camp cooking.

The late Colonel Charles Goodnight, a famed pioneer rancher of the northwest Texas plains, tried for years to convince others that buffalo crossed with domestic cattle make a superior meat. Goodnight raised dozens of the beasts and reportedly dined almost exclusively on the meat and bread. He lived well in a hard country for almost one hundred years.

Despite Goodnight's failure to find a market for his "beefalo," game remains a prime prospect of saving the economic hides of many ranchers. The huge Y-O Ranch west of Kerrville has a flourishing year-round business charging hunters to shoot exotic animals. So do many others.

The big King Ranch of South Texas may have found a way to relieve world hunger with nilgai (correct) antelopes it brought from India in 1929. The Associated Press reported from Kingsville that the original herd of a dozen antelope has exploded into an estimated twenty thousand by 1985.

"They're big and have no natural predators here," said Dr. Rod Ward of the Kleberg Wildlife Research Center at Texas A.&I. University. "Like all wild animals they're basically immune to disease.

"These animals are healthy, prevalent, and breed the year-round. They're already eating ranchers out of house and home."

Dr. Ward suggested a study of ways to market the animals as a cheap source of meat for the poor. Meat offered from some nilgai sold rapidly at prices averaging $1.85 a pound — less than comparable cuts of beef. Texas A&M University tests showed the meat to be lean and nutritious, containing much less fat and cholesterol than beef, the AP reported. Ward added the meat has a palatable flavor. Adult nilgai averaged 206 pounds weight.

Hunters and even longtime ranchers are discovering that

old bucks and long-bearded turkey toms are hardly in the class with younger specimens and females when served on the dining table. The main purpose served by big-horned trophies and old toms is they look better in photographs or mounted as decoration.

Nothing deflates the Male Ego more than to have his kill rejected by the person he wants most to please — his wife. Just as disappointing to both parties is cooking game without knowing how.

Properly dressed and cooked, it becomes a soul-satisfying product of hunting prowess and culinary art. Ignorance — which this book seeks to help overcome — has spoiled such bliss too many times. The harvesting and cooking of game is a wonderful world of its own.

Approach the subject with an open mind. Hunting usually requires great patience and skill, and often the would-be target walks or flies away as the winner. The outdoors increasingly beckon modern America of both sexes, both the primitive and sophisticated senses.

The hunter must learn how to take care of his kill. It is wasteful and unkind to shoot any animal just for its horns and hide when the carcass is good food.

Forget all you ever learned about cooking domestic meat. Never tell a game cook: "This is good. It tastes like beef." Wild game varieties have fine eating qualities and flavors all their own and any comparison with domestic meat insults the skilled game cook. Many recipes can be adjusted to good use on either wild or domestic meat.

Although part of wild game's high food value results from its feeding on natural food, much of its diet often comes from a farmer's corn or oat crop or maize fields which have become pheasant and quail habitat in northwest Texas.

Living in a climate hostile to domestic livestock, Alaskans are modern leaders in using game for human consumption. The biggest state is famous for its abundance of game. Even so, reindeer imported from Siberia are being raised domestically for food and demand reportedly exceeds the supply.

Research in Alaska indicates lean venison contains less than half the calories of a similar portion of trimmed beef or pork, and that venison grown in the wild has higher protein and vitamin content.

Research in Great Britain, New Zealand, and elsewhere, has produced similar findings, although more scientific evidence is needed before domestic livestock producers and most consumers will accept wild game as important food.

The Texas Parks and Wildlife Department is a solid, well-run agency. Yet its data on nutritional value of game is sketchy. As early as 1979, however, its magazine reported:

"Wild game usually has higher amounts of useable protein than domestic meat. It also has fewer calories and less fat. Venison has fifteen percent fewer calories, fifty percent more protein and sixty percent less fat than an equal portion of beef.

"Although wild pheasant has twenty-two percent less protein than domestic roast turkey, it also has twenty-five percent fewer calories and thirty-eight percent less fat."

The prestigious *New England Journal of Medicine* in 1985 proclaimed that cavemen ate healthier diets than modern Americans. These primitives ate game, birds, fish, and wild plants. This was a low-fat, high-protein, low-salt, high-fiber diet, free of chemicals and additives. If that sounds familiar today, remember the cave people learned it first.

True, the average ancient died younger than those today. Death came early to them from accidents, weather, plague and diseases, many of which can be treated or prevented today. But the old-timers did have healthier digestive systems, the reports indicate.

In 1972, when Encino Press published the original *Texas Wild Game Cookbook,* the authors wrote:

"This cookbook on the handling and cooking of wild game is offered in the belief that tons of delicious meat and possibly hundreds of marriages can be saved each year through the experience and knowledge the authors herewith share with others."

The ensuing years have developed additional knowledge.

For hunters without a willing cook, welfare agencies prepare and serve tons of wild game to the poor.

As one old-timer remarked about whiskey: "There's no such thing as bad whiskey. Just some is better than others."

The widespread use of home freezers has given many families a year-around supply of game for the table. One result has been a decline in the number of locker plants to process game, although these are still found in all principal hunting areas. Processing prices have increased too. Central Texas deer seldom produce more than fifty pounds of dressed meat apiece, often less, yet the price of commercial processing has risen to thirty dollars or forty dollars per animal. Such processors can make sausage or smoke the meat. A growing number of hunters dress their own kill, with excellent results.

The hurrying person misses much of hunting's pleasure — which is far more than shooting and killing. Many "hunters" never carry a firearm even if they go afield. Socializing in the cabin or tent is perhaps the most enjoyable part. Getting away from the tensions of "civilized" life is a major reason to head for the hills.

One old-timer in Edwards County refused to take a hunting trip of less than a week's duration.

"A man who can't stay a week ain't got time to go huntin'," said he.

This individual never even carried a rifle on the first day. He "made camp" and scouted the area. If he did or did not kill a deer during the week, he was satisfied and went home richly rewarded.

Most city dwellers who hunt are weekend hunters, although many manage several trips a year.

Deer have become so abundant in the Southwest, particularly in the Texas hill country, that the Texas Parks and Wildlife Commission in 1985 extended the season from November 9 to January 5 (generally) and increased the whitetail limit to four deer per season, with a maximum of two bucks. The license also permits one mule deer a year. Some variations are made by counties so check before killing.

Until a quarter-century ago, killing female deer or spike (one-prong) bucks was against the law. Now these are on the most-wanted list for controlling herds to reduce over-population, under-nourishment, and die-offs of deer.

A trace of cavalier prejudice persists against killing these tender things. If you want the best eating: take does and spikes.

Lest inexperienced folks low-rate the skill of doe-hunting, let it be recorded that the female of the species becomes just as wild as the male when the shooting starts. Females are also more suspicious of man. If fed, deer can be attracted to certain areas but they never become domesticated.

Our personal record deer for years of hunting is a nine-point whitetail from the rocky hills of Edwards county. It looked like an elephant in size through the four-power telescope of a .30/06 rifle. We went for help and our generous fellow-loader estimated the buck weighed 115 pounds field-dressed. We guessed 125 pounds.

The buck actually weighed ninety-seven pounds, large by hill country standards. Deer in South Texas and the Trans-Pecos average larger size than those of more crowded habitat.

Care of a carcass after killing is highly important, and requires foresight.

Field-dressing is done usually in the area where the deer is killed. Some landowners request that the operation be performed in camp where the insides can be disposed of in a designated place. Some hunters believe that leaving entrails from a dead deer makes other deer avoid the area. This is questionable but it does attract coyotes, raccoons, skunks, opossum and other varmints.

Although this is not a manual on how to dress a deer, here's a helpful hint that may horrify the he-man hunter: Take along waterproof surgical or gardening gloves. These help keep hands, clothing and carcass clean.

Hang the deer as soon as possible in a cool shady place, screened from flies. If possible, carcasses should be hung outside overnight to cool. Rain will not harm the meat. This hunter prefers early skinning of the carcass, allowing it to "cure" better. We also hang it head-down, which improves meat quality.

Experts disagree on whether to wash freshly-killed game. One old theory is that washing increases the chance of spoilage. We favor washing the carcass, particularly if it isn't well-shot. Unless the weather is cool to cold, refrigerate your game at the first opportunity. Deer can be quartered and packed into ice chests easily if a refrigerator isn't handy. Take large plastic bags or wrapping on your hunting trip.

We hold a theory which others may dispute. We believe a deer killed with a "slow" rifle such as a .30-30 caliber (old-fashioned type) often tastes better than one felled with a later-model, more high-powered weapon. Granted the newer models are more deadly and less likely to wound a deer without killing it. Any animal hit with such an explosive charge, unless you are one of those deadly hit-'em-in-the-neck marksmen, sometimes leaves the carcass bloodshot.

This may be imagination, but the best-tasting venison we ever had was killed with an old .25−35 saddle carbine, cousin to the .30-30. The .25−35 is also splendid for shooting turkeys. With it you can kill a turkey without destroying the carcass.

We select a rifle according to time of day. For afternoons and evenings, a high-power weapon is preferred. It is less likely to wound an animal which may not be found until the next day. For mornings, a slower rifle is fine. If the mortally-wounded prey runs into the woods, you have time to find it before dark.

Our .30/06 has some advantages. But we can relate a sad (but true) story of knocking down a nice buck with a shot through the neck at close range (he was peering over the edge of a cliff behind me). We climbed the cliff, found the motionless deer spread flat on the rocks with a hole in his neck. As we approached to field-dress the animal, minus rifle, he rolled over the cliff and ran out of the country.

Our high-speed bullet hadn't hit a vital spot; just passed through the flesh and temporarily paralyzed the animal. This wouldn't have happened with an old .30-30, whose neck wound was always fatal. Once we killed a small buck, which was hiding behind a cedar tree with a .25−35. The bullet from a high-speed rifle would have exploded and spun off before reaching its target.

Another tip on dressing deer:

Experts increasingly use hind-quarters of deer and other animals almost as backstrap. Remove the long muscle whole, utilizing knife and fingers. All "white" portions are thrown away — fat, bone, and connecting tissue. The remaining red meat is more tender and delicious than the usual cut. It goes well as cutlets.

At a locker plant deer ordinarily remain in coolers for several days and sometimes are skinned by local taxidermists who sell the hides and mount the heads for a fee. Hides removed in camp bring a dollar or so each from fur buyers, if you can find one. Unless several skins are to be delivered, it's hardly worth the effort to sell hides even though fine leather can be manufactured from them.

In the past, we have been able to arrange for tanning of some deer hides. We like the natural gray-white finish best, but the leather can be dyed any color and made into durable, attractive gloves or jackets. Javelina leather makes strikingly beautiful gloves.

Although dressed game increasingly is being preserved in home freezers, a locker plant will cut up the carcass and package it according to the hunter's instructions. While this may be presumptuous, give thought to what you will do with a deer if you get one. It helps to give locker plant workers written instructions, for such places become scenes of pandemonium during their busy hours.

With just two in our family living at home, we order venison put into small packages, one or two pounds, of sausage or chili. The usual packaging at commercial places is about a four-person quantity.

A variety of cuts are available. Hams can be left whole for baking, barbecuing or smoking. They can be sliced into round steak or divided into roasts. Backstraps and tenders (there are two of each) can be packaged whole or cut into (T-bone) chops.

Shoulders (less meaty than hams) can be made into steaks or roasts or ground into sausage, hamburger, chili meat, or other purposes described in the menus which follow. Some cooks barbecue or bake ribs of game animals. While not very meaty, ribs are delicious. Rib and flank meat is great for fajitas.

We are not barbecue enthusiasts and find this method usually too dry for the best cooking of lean meat such as venison. We have eaten tasty barbecued game but this may represent tasty sauce rather than the cooking. One can eat a shingle with the right sauce.

VENISON

If your hunter brings home a trophy buck and you are expected to make it tasty, have the backstrap removed for cooking and perhaps the hams. Grind the remainder for chili, hamburger and sausage.

There are two important grinds of venison. The coarse chili grind is useful not only for chili but for the meat in spaghetti sauce. The regular fine grind of venison can be used in any way that ground beef or pork can be used. The ground meat makes wonderful sausage. Usually it is mixed with pork but sometimes with ground beef. Once we had an entire buck made into sausage, using one-half pork.

Texas has locker plants where sausage-making is a fine art. Many plants have sausage specialties. We have enjoyed smoked, links and pan sausage. It is all delicious. For those who would like to make their own sausage we include recipes.

Use the fine grind of venison in venisonburgers, meat balls, pizzas and most especially in the "skillet dinners" now on convenience food shelves. Any of the packaged dinners is improved using ground venison in place of beef.

These are especially handy at a ranch or camp where an electric skillet is the principal means of cooking.

Properly dressed and cooked, every part of a young buck or tender doe makes fine eating. These can be cut into roasts, chops, hams and ground meat. The backstrap can be cooked as simply or as gourmet as you prefer. Except for the very choice tender cuts, though, venison must be cooked moist.

Since most venison will come frozen from the processor,

locker or deep-freeze, it is very good to thaw it in buttermilk. This has a tenderizing effect and if you fry or smother the meat you have a built-in batter. Dip the meat thawed in buttermilk in seasoned flour and brown in the skillet in fat. Pour off excess fat, add water or wine, cover and steam until tender.

The addition of vinegar, cooking wine or lemon juice to the water in which the meat is thawed also has a tenderizing effect.

Another simple way to start venison is to parboil in one or two cans of bouillon, depending on the amount of meat, and then treat as any other meat to fry, bake or broil.

The simplest way to cook venison or most game is in a skillet, oven or barbecue grill. There are now on the market new (or very old) cooking utensils that cook at very high temperatures or very low and game comes out moist and tender without drying.

The CLAY POT is found in many specialty stores. Some are glazed which makes clean-up easier. The shapes vary from round to oblong and from small to large enough to hold a twelve-pound turkey. The great advantage of the clay pot is that the game cooks at high temperature but remains moist. No pre-browning is necessary and no fat is used. However, the clay pot MUST be soaked in water at least fifteen minutes before putting it in a cold oven. The temperature then should be raised to 425 degrees F. for venison and game birds. Check your roast for doneness. A large one should take about two hours.

The CROCK-POT has become the best friend of the busy cook. A meal left to cook slowly in the morning is ready to serve at night without overcooking. Venison roast must be browned in hot fat and seasoned before it is added to vegetables in the crock-pot for slow cooking.

This method is especially good for skinned geese, ducks and wild turkey breast. Chili made by this method is also very satisfactory.

The PRESSURE COOKER is one of my favorite utensils for making sure game of undetermined tenderness is made moist and palatable.

The first venison we ate in Austin was prepared by Katy Walker who cooked for William M. (Tudey) Thornton, a longtime *Dallas News* Capitol Correspondent and avid hunter.

Katy took a roast or ham and scored it to the bone. This made slices for serving that were seasoned completely. She salted, peppered and floured the meat and browned it in fat. In the same roaster or heavy skillet made a flour gravy and added slices of onions and lots of sliced celery. She returned the roast to the gravy, covered and steamed or baked until tender. The roast was delicious and the gravy even better, especially served over rice. Katy always served spaghetti with venison, and made this with a tomato sauce.

We like an oven-barbecued roast or ham. The meat may be thawed in water into which a couple of tablespoons of vinegar are added.

Score the meat to the bone so that seasoning may penetrate or pierce with a knife. Insert slivers of fat bacon and slivers of garlic. (The experts say that the larding may be done with a veterinarian's needle, but we have never seen one.) Place the meat in a roaster or in foil and add any variation of the following sauce.

1 or 2 sticks of butter or oleo (Depending on size of roast)
   Juice of one lemon and add a few slices to the pan
$\frac{1}{4}$ cup of brown sugar

2 tablespoons of prepared mustard
1 bottle of Worcestershire or catsup or soy sauce (this flavor depends on your taste)

Place all of the above ingredients in a small sauce pan with one-half cup of water and simmer a few minutes. Baste meat with this sauce for about 30 minutes at a temperature of 450 degrees, then enclose in foil or cover in roaster with remaining sauce and cook slowly for several hours at 300 degrees.

Our former cook, Sally Ann, made a variation of this sauce using oleo or butter:

$\frac{1}{2}$ cup of vinegar
$\frac{1}{2}$ cup of finely chopped onion
1 bottle of catsup
1 teaspoon of salt

1 teaspoon of black pepper
2 teaspoon of prepared mustard (if desired) (enough water to make medium thin sauce)

VENISON

VENISON ROAST

Take knife and insert bacon and garlic into roast. Make the following marinade:

1 medium carrot, grated	2 bay leaves
1 cup of chopped onion	¹/₂ teaspoon of salt
¹/₂ cup of chopped parsley	¹/₂ teaspoon of pepper
¹/₂ cup of diced celery	6 whole cloves

Put half of the above in baking pan. Place roast on the vegetables and cover with the other half. Pour over this 2 cups of oil and 3 cups of dry white wine. Marinate for two days in the refrigerator, turning meat several times.

Roast and baste with marinade at 350 degrees until tender.

Mrs. Pat Crockett, Bryan

VENISON ROAST WITH PORK ROAST OR HAM

My friend Willie Bolander always cooks venison roast with fresh pork roast. I find a smoked pork ham or shoulder imparts a wonderful flavor to the venison if cooked together.

Venison ham or roast

Smoked pork ham or shoulder.

Salt, pepper and garlic seasoned bacon strips.

Season the venison with salt, pepper and with a knife cut slits in the meat and insert bacon strips that have been seasoned either with slivers of garlic or garlic salt.

Place the smoked ham and venison together in a roaster and cook at 350 degrees for twenty minutes per pound for the TOTAL weight. Remove, slice and serve. Be prepared for compliments.

Do not use a cooked, boned ham for this mixture. A small, smoked pork shoulder is sufficient.

ROAST VENISON IN BLACK COFFEE GRAVY

Take a venison ham or shoulder and score the meat to the bone. Insert slices of bacon seasoned with garlic powder into the cuts in the roast. Sliced fresh onions or slivers of garlic may be used if desired.

Place the roast in a glass or granite bowl and pour over it

one cup of vinegar or white wine. Cover and refrigerate overnight.

When ready to cook, pour off the liquid, brown in a heavy pot with a small amount of fat until well browned. Pour two cups of strong black coffee over the roast, and two cups of water, cover with a tight lid and cook slowly until meat is tender. It may take several hours depending on the age of the animal. Add more water in small amounts as necessary.

Season with salt and pepper in the final few minutes of cooking.

Thicken the gravy with one tablespoon of flour if desired, or serve unthickened from the pot.

The Crock-pot is a good utensil for this recipe.

ROAST VENISON

Hope the roast is from a deer in excellent condition. Use your old reliable Dutch oven or a roasting pan with a tight lid.

Salt and pepper your roast, be it rump or shoulder. Do not flour. Use water sparingly. Cook at low temperature in the oven for a long while, depending on the size of your roast. Best use your meat thermometer as rare venison is not as good as well done.

Clara Louise Cape, San Marcos

EARLY TEXAS CHILI RECIPE

This is a pioneer recipe for real Texas chili, from the peppers up.

"Hunt until you find old-fashioned dry, large, red peppers. Wipe them clean with a moist rag — remove seeds. Place in shallow baking tins and dry them in extremely low heated oven until crisp. Remove from oven and cool. Put them through meat-grinder and you will have chili powder to which you may add the herbs of which you are most fond or none at all. One usually adds a pinch of garlic and/or onion. Use tomatoes, canned. I use Ro-Tel, instead of water. Simmer before adding your already cooked or sautéed chunks of venison (at least two pounds). Cook slowly for several hours (simmer). Add a small amount of cooking oil or margarine. Should you prefer your chili thicker, just sprinkle in a little corn meal and stir."

Clara Louise Cape, San Marcos

VENISON CHILI

Make chili in at least two pound lots since it keeps well and can be used in a dozen ways.

My two-pound portions of chili-ground venison are frozen as hard as a rock. The meat thaws and cooks at the same time if it is placed in the pressure cooker with a modest amount of water and boiled until thawed. Pressure cook it twenty minutes. Since venison is all lean meat, it becomes tender without melting. To the pressure cooked venison, I add Wick Fowler's chili mix [2-Alarm Chili] and cook to the thickness of our liking. Fowler Chili Mix is approximately

5 tablespoons of chili powder	1 teaspoon dehydrated onion
1 tablespoon of ground oregano	1 teaspoon dehydrated garlic
2 teaspoons of salt	1 teaspoon paprika

Amber package of ground hot pepper we omit as too hot for our innards. Many like their chili HOT. To the cooked meat, add one eight-ounce can of tomato sauce and the above spices. Fowler includes about four tablespoons of Masa flour to make a pourable thickener at the end, but we don't use that either although some others do.

VENISON CHILI-DIP

For every pound of venison used to make a batch of chili, add a pound of grated sharp cheese and warm until the cheese melts.

Serve with corn chips. This is wonderful in your chafing dish for wintertime parties.

STUFFED PEPPERS — VENISON CHILI

Parboil half of a bell pepper for each guest. Place in flat baking dish and add hominy. Cover with Venison Chili; chopped or sliced onions and bake for 30 minutes at 350 degrees F. Add grated cheese the last 15 minutes or until cheese melts. Serve with green salad and tortillas.

VENISON

VENISON STROGANOFF

3 tablespoons butter
1/2 cup chopped onion
1 small clove garlic, minced
1/4 cup regular all purpose
    flour
1 teaspoon salt
1/2 teaspoon dill weed

1 can (10 1/2 ounces)
    condensed beef broth
1 can (2 ounces) sliced
    mushrooms
2 cups cooked venison
1 cup plain yogurt at room
    temperature

In large skillet melt butter; sauté onion and garlic until onion is tender. Stir in flour, salt and dill weed. Remove from heat; gradually stir in beef broth and mushrooms with liquid. Cook over medium heat, stirring constantly, until thickened.

Add venison, heat over low heat five to ten minutes. Stir in yogurt; heat to serving temperature. (Do not boil.) Serve over rice or noodles. Makes four to six servings. If you use noodles, use the large flat ones, cook in salted boiling water and drain, don't rinse.

VENISON WITH SOUR CREAM

1 or 2 pounds of venison cut
    in cubes
1 teaspoon caraway seed
2 bouillon cubes in 2 cups of
    water
1 onion, chopped fine

Juice of one-half lemon
2 cups sour cream
1/4 cup (one stick) butter or
    cooking oil
Flour, salt and pepper

Brown meat cubes in butter or oil. Season. Dredge in flour. Add caraway, onion, lemon juice, cream and bouillon cubes in water.

Cook one and one half hours in a heavy skillet. Serve on toast.

VENISON

BURGUNDY VENISON

2 pounds venison, round	$^1/_4$ teaspoon marjoram
1 garlic clove	$^1/_4$ teaspoon oregano
3 medium onions	$^1/_2$ cup burgundy wine
4 tablespoons butter	$^1/_2$ pint sour cream
Salt, pepper, flour	4 ounce can mushrooms
	(optional)

Cut venison into one-inch cubes. Tenderize and set aside. Sauté garlic, onions and butter until soft and brown. Remove onions and garlic from pan. Brown venison slowly in drippings. Return onions and garlic to pan. Add flour and water to thicken gravy. Add salt and pepper. Simmer $1^1/_2$ hours.

Add mushrooms, herbs and wine. Simmer 15 minutes. Add sour cream and serve over wild rice. Serves six.

VENISON ROULADEN

20 slices of lean venison, $^1/_8$ inch thick	Mustard
	2 cups of bacon, chopped fine
1 cup sour pickles chopped fine	$^1/_4$ cup sour cream
	1 tablespoon flour

On each slice of meat: Spread mustard thin. Salt and pepper lightly. Spread pickles thin. Place about 2 teaspoons of bacon on pickles. Roll meat slices, place in bottom of enameled roast pan, cover. In 325° oven, bake 40–45 minutes.

Remove meat from pan. Dress gravy with sour cream, flour, mixed with $^1/_2$ cup of water. Add 1 teaspoon soy sauce, salt and pepper to taste. If desired omit sour cream and use 2 tablespoons of flour to dress gravy.

Kim Campbell

VENISON LOG

MIX:
- ½ teaspoon liquid smoke
- ¼ teaspoon onion powder
- ⅛ teaspoon garlic powder
- 2 tablespoons Morton's Tender Quick-Meat Cure

ADD:
- 2 pounds lean ground venison

Form into 3 logs — 2 inches by 6 inches. Wrap in plastic wrap and refrigerate for 24 hours. Remove wrap and place on rack in pan.

Bake at 300 degrees for 1 hour and 45 minutes. Do not substitute for meat cure.

Kay Campbell
District food show winner in Wichita Falls — 1978

MY FAVORITE VENISON CHOPS

Thaw any chops or round steak in buttermilk.

Dip moist slices in seasoned flour and brown in pressure cooker, lid off. Remove chops from fat, pour off any excess and brown one chopped onion and four ribs of celery in the fat and drippings. Add enough water to make a medium thin gravy. More flour may be needed and be sure to use the seasoned flour that you dipped the chops in before browning.

Return the browned chops to the gravy and pressure cook for 15–20 minutes. Any cut of venison is tender and tasty cooked in this manner, and the gravy is great on cooked rice, noodles or if you can stand the calories try hot biscuits.

Fruit salad, green salad or the kraut relish served with this chop and gravy dinner is complete.

SACHTLEBEN VENISON CASSEROLE

Take 1–1½ pounds boned venison steak, cut in bite-size pieces. Season with salt and pepper. Turn in flour.

Brown in skillet with 3 tablespoons of butter.

Remove meat from pan.

Add one tablespoon of butter and 3 tablespoons of flour to drippings in pan. Brown.

Add 3 cups of water and one small minced onion.

VENISON

19

(Optional) Add 1 small can of mushrooms.
(Optional) Add 1 or 2 cloves of garlic.
Season to taste with salt and pepper.
Add venison and stir into baking dish.
Cook (simmer) in oven at low temperature for 1–1¹/₂ hours.
Serve over steamed rice or noodles. Should serve four to six.
This is also good over cornbread.

Laura Walser, Blanco

GAME BARBECUE

1. Mix one third each:
   salt, pepper, chili powder (keep in large shaker or jar with punctured top)
2. Sprinkle on thawed meat generously the night before. Let meat set at room temperature till time to cook.
3. Barbecue at low temperature. Keep meat away from coals, no direct heat. Oak, hickory or mesquite wood for smoke and flavor 8–12 hours.
4. Meat will gain a "varnish" that seals it. Use meat thermometer to determine doneness. It can be served rare.
5 .Barbecued meat can be frozen. One to as many as six deer hams at once — turkey — even doves.

The Reverend Richard E. McCabe, Austin

QUICHE UVALDE (Apologies to Lorraine)

Cook ³/₄ to one pound of venison sausage. (Cool and crumble and store in refrigerator.) Cook 9 or 10 inch pastry shell for 10 minutes at 350 degrees. Scald 1 cup heavy cream. Set aside.

In a bowl beat three eggs until light and fluffy. Add ¹/₄ teaspoon ground mustard and hot cream. Continue beating until light and foamy.

Grate 10-inch brick of Swiss cheese or use Mozzarella cheese — already grated.

Into the browned pastry crust, sprinkle basil liberally, and dried chives sparsely — or add sliced sweet onions sautéed in butter. Cover with sausage, then cover sausage with cheese.

Pour cream mixture over cheese. Shake nutmeg over the top. Bake at 350 degrees for 30 minutes.

Great served hot.

VENISON ANGOSTURA STEW

2 pounds boneless venison
    cut in 1-inch cubes
Salt and pepper
¼ cup butter or margarine
1 large onion, chopped
1 garlic clove, chopped

1 cup of tomato or V-8 juice
1 cup orange juice
1 tablespoon Angostura Bitters
1 8-ounce package of mixed,
    dried fruits

Sprinkle meat cubes with salt, pepper and flour. Heat butter or margarine in heavy skillet or Dutch oven. Brown meat on all sides. Add onions, garlic, tomato and orange juice, Angostura Bitters and the dried fruit. Cover tightly and simmer 1½ to 2 hours or until meat is tender. If necessary, add small amounts of water or red wine from time to time. When meat is done, thicken by stirring in a mixture of 1 tablespoon of flour in 1 cup of water or 1 tablespoon of cornstarch in 1 cup of water. Taste and adjust for salt and pepper seasoning.

Garth Jones, Austin

VENISON

BEERY DEER STEW
(adapted from Flemish beef stew or Carbonnade Flamande)

4 slices bacon, cut in one-inch pieces (smoked, thick slice is best)
2 pounds lean venison (such as round steak) cut in one-inch chunks
1 bay leaf
2 onions, sliced thick
1 tablespoon flour
1 can of beer (cook's choice)
1 beef bouillon cube dissolved in one cup of water
2 teaspoons brown sugar
2 teaspoons vinegar
1 teaspoon thyme
1 tablespoon parsley
Salt
Coarse ground pepper
4 carrots, sliced diagonally
4 medium potatoes (or less) in about one-inch cubes

In Dutch oven or electric skillet fry bacon until crisp. Set aside. Brown venison cubes in bacon fat. Add flour and stir until meat is coated and all flour absorbed.

Add beer, bouillon, onions, brown sugar, vinegar, thyme, salt and pepper and simmer covered for about an hour until meat is almost tender. Add water a little at a time if necessary (or beer from the can in your hand).

For last 30 minutes of cooking add carrots, potatoes, and parsley and simmer until tender.

Correct seasoning if necessary. Garnish with crisp bacon.

Serves four to six, more or less.

Remarks: It is even better if the venison is marinated overnight in the beer, bay leaf, onions, etc. Just let it dry off a few minutes before browning. And it will add flavor to the stew if you add a clove of garlic, minced, while cooking.

The whole thing freezes fine and actually tastes better the second day after cooking.

Garth Jones, Austin

VENIBOB
(Shish kebab with venison)

If you don't tell your guests what they are eating they will compliment you on the taste of the succulent beef they have eaten. Tell them afterwards. A good ploy is to bring the talk about food around to meats and inevitably someone will say how they cannot stand venison. With a straight face tell them that's what they have just eaten and pronounced so delicious.

Procedure:
Marinade —

2 cups red wine (burgundy or sherry or Chianti)
6 tablespoons lemon juice
1 onion
3 cloves garlic, finely chopped (if using garlic juice — 1 tablespoon)
6 bay leaves
1 tablespoon allspice

Let ingredients soak in marinade for a couple of hours at room temperature before putting in meat.

Any cut of venison will do. Slice pieces of meat into $1-1\frac{1}{2}$ inch square pieces (don't be too particular about size and shape). Rinse meat well; soak in marinade for at least two hours; take meat out and dry meat with paper towel. Put on skewer and barbecue over very hot flame. Object is to cook outside crisp while maintaining tender interior of meat. Ideally for Venibob, use 14-inch or longer skewer. Alternate small white onion, large mushroom, meat, slices of green pepper, small cherry tomato, meat, etc. Before putting over coals brush meat well with melted butter in which has been mixed one-half teaspoon paprika and about the same amount of black pepper. Some connoisseurs put a thin strip of bacon over the top of the Venibob and let it drip down as it is cooking.

Ira Iscoe, Austin

SWEDISH MEAT BALLS
Made with Venison

$\frac{1}{2}$ pound ground venison
$\frac{1}{2}$ pound of ground pork
$\frac{1}{8}$ teaspoon each of ginger, nutmeg and allspice
1 beaten egg
1 tablespoon minced onion
$\frac{1}{2}$ cup of bread crumbs
Salt and pepper to taste

Mix together and shape in small round balls. Brown in lightly oiled skillet. Cover with water, cover with a tight lid and simmer at low heat for 30—40 minutes. This makes 4—5 servings.

Florence Olsen, Austin

VENISONBURGERS

1 pound fine-ground venison
  Salt and pepper to taste
3 tablespoons canned milk

Add as your taste dictates:
Onion salt
Garlic salt
Prepared mustard
One egg, slightly beaten

Form into patties and broil in skillet greased slightly with butter. You may prefer to cook over charcoal. Serve on buns with lettuce, tomatoes and sliced pickle.

We have friends who like a venison patty for breakfast, omitting the onion, garlic seasoning, etc.

VENISON PIZZAS

1 pound of ground venison or
   venison sausage
  Salt and pepper to taste
1 can of biscuits

1 can of pizza sauce
Grated cheese, sharp or
  Mozzarella
Sliced mushrooms, olives or
  sliced fresh onions

Cook venison or sausage in skillet and drain. Slices of link sausage may be used. Season meat if needed.

Roll out canned biscuits in small pizza rounds. Place on a cookie or pizza sheet. Spread with 1 tablespoon of pizza sauce. Add venison and garnish. Top with cheese and broil about 10 to 15 minutes in hot oven. This makes about 16 miniature pizzas.

VENISON MINCEMEAT
(any ground venison)

2 pounds cooked venison, chopped in food grinder	$^3/_4$ pounds chopped suet or butter
4 pounds chopped apple	$^1/_2$ teaspoon cloves
2 pounds raisins	1 teaspoon mace
4 cups either brown or white sugar	$^1/_2$ teaspoon nutmeg
	2 teaspoon salt
	$1^1/_2$ teaspoon cinnamon

Add cider to cover mixture. If cider is not available, use fruit juices or water with one-half cup vinegar. Sweet fruit juices reduce the amount of sugar required.

Cook very slowly until the fruits are tender (about one hour). Makes ten pints.

VENISON (Onion, Butter and Bouillon)

1 pound of thawed venison chops	1 large onion, sliced
1 stick of butter	1 can of beef bouillon

Brown onion in butter but do not burn. Flour, salt and pepper venison and brown in grease in a separate skillet.

Add venison to onion and butter in skillet. Add 1 can bouillon. Cover and steam until done.

VENISON SAUSAGE

Elgin Burrer, an Austin man of Fredericksburg–German ancestry, makes sausage as follows:

Take two parts sausage-ground venison and mix with one part ground beef brisket. Salt and pepper and add freshly ground garlic. Avoid sage.

Smoke for two weeks and put up in casings. This will keep almost indefinitely. The flavor and keeping quality both can be improved by hanging the smoked sausage awhile in a protected cool dry place, such as a carport or porch.

Another Burrer recipe is for preparing ground venison without making it into sausage, as follows:

Mix one-half ground venison with one-quarter beef brisket

VENISON 25

and one-quarter ground fresh pork ham. Put into two-pound packages and smoke for two weeks. This may be seasoned after thawing. The meat can be used as hamburger or any other groundmeat purpose. It avoids rancid fat and will keep a long time.

JERKY

Hikers and outdoor buffs today are learning about Jerky, a dry-preserved meat of primitive man and pioneers before refrigeration was invented.

Jerky and its near-relative Pemmican can be made from almost any lean red meat — venison, elk, beef, or javelina.

Dressing the meat is highly important, to eliminate fat and gristle which may turn rancid. Removal of the "white" from such red meat also leaves the tender and nutritious muscle minus its toughest portions. Any long muscle will do for Jerky, cut into strips about six inches long and half an inch thick. David Baxter, in *Texas Parks and Wildlife Magazine*, advises where to go from there:

Place the meat in a bowl or dish that can be covered. After the first layer of meat, sprinkle it liberally with hickory smoke salt and a touch of garlic or onion salt for seasoning. Add black pepper if you like it hot, or any other favorite spice such as oregano, marjoram, basil and thyme. Fill the bowl with layers of seasoned meat.

Cover the dish and place it in the refrigerator for at least eight hours, to give salt and seasoning time to permeate the meat with a hearty flavor.

Next, blanch the meat in a pan of water to destroy surface bacteria. For each quart of water add one tablespoon of salt. Bring water to a simmer. Dip each strip of meat in the water and hold it there about fifteen seconds. The meat will then turn whitish-gray.

Place strips of meat on a cookie sheet and heat in oven at lowest possible heat for six to sixteen hours — or until the meat is coal black outside and dark and dry throughout. Leave the oven door ajar (this is important) so moisture can escape. The slow heat dehydrates the meat, and when it cools it is ready to eat.

Jerky has about ten to fifteen percent moisture content. Ten pounds of meat will make about three and a half pounds of Jerky — which is not only lighter but much less bulky than the original cut. Old-timers carried Jerky in their saddlebags, and it is just as tasty and handy strapped to your bike.

Kept dry in a covered jar away from insects, Jerky will last for weeks. If you have a refrigerator handy, store the jar there until ready to travel. The meat will last almost indefinitely this way.

Mr. Baxter adds that a traditionalist with plenty of free time will season his Jerky in brine, and do the cooking on a slow outdoor fire. This is picturesque and aromatic as done by the Mexican-American *vaqueros* (and their families) in the brush country of Southwest Texas, but is hardly suited to the city game cook.

The pioneer method calls for a solution composed of five cups of water to each cup of salt. Soak the raw meat for about fifteen minutes. Drain. Then "cure" the strips for a week or ten days over a low smoky fire (keep dogs away). The fire should not be hot enough to cook the meat, which needs to be covered each night during the processing.

Pemmican, eaten mainly in cold climates, contains fat which is absent from Jerky.

The Baxter recipe calls for pounding a quantity of Jerky until it is shredded. Render cubes of animal fat over a low fire — without boiling the grease. Mix equal quantities of shredded Jerky and hot fat. Pack in commercial casings or waterproof bags.

Excessively dry Jerky will crumble, but is tasty served with milk gravy, or mixed in a skillet with flour and vegetables.

Many meat counters now sell Jerky made usually from beef. Made from game, this old-timer is just as tasty and, in our opinion, more nutritious. It also provides a neighborhood conversation bit if you smoke it over a slow fire in your backyard.

VENISON BACKSTRAP

The backstrap is the venison tenderloin.

It may be sliced thin and broiled in butter rapidly.

It may be cut in $1\frac{1}{2}$ inch thick slices, wrapped in bacon and broiled like a filet mignon.

One of the most elegant ways to cook the backstrap is simply to season it with salt and pepper, wrap the whole thing round and round with bacon and roast in your oven. It can be sliced at the table in any thickness.

Doris Herring cooked venison backstrap in this manner:

Season heavily, mainly red pepper. Cover with sliced onions and bay leaf. Marinate in red wine and Worcestershire at least 12 hours; overnight is better.

Wrap in bacon, cook in a fast oven at 450 degrees for 35 to 40 minutes. Use a meat thermometer and cook to "BEEF" well-done.

VENISON PICANTE

Cut slices of venison backstrap $^3/_8 - ^1/_2$ inch thick and pound each slice three or four times on each side with a wide tooth meat mallet to increase tenderness. Soak pounded meat in milk for 5 – 10 minutes and then dredge while wet with milk in a mixture of flour, salt and pepper. Spread picante sauce (Pace's Original preferred) on one slice of meat and top with another slice. Gently tap the "Sandwich" around the edge with a mallet to seal in the sauce.

Fry in $^1/_2$ inches very hot bacon fat or fry oil of your choice until well done and serve hot. Note: Slices of venison ham are suitable substitute for backstrap provided the inner layers of tough gristle are removed.

Patricia K. White, Uvalde

SAUTEED VENISON BACKSTRAP

Slice tenderloin into $^3/_4$ inches and pound flat. Dredge in flour and sauté in hot butter. Remove meat from pan. To the juices in the pan add:

2 diced shallots
1 cup of dry white wine and reduce volume by one half

ADD:
4 ounces beef stock and bring to simmer
2 tablespoons Dijon mustard
1 tablespoon horseradish

Serve over venison slices. The horseradish is the secret ingredient.

Adapted from a recipe of Chef John Randall
Austin Headliners Club

VENISON FOR THE VENTURESOME

USE ONLY PARTS UNDAMAGED BY THE SHOOTING AND
FRESH FROM THE KILL

VENISON BRAINS AND EGGS

Parboil brains for about five minutes in salted water. Pour into
colander and cool under running water. Remove any mem-
brane. Break and stir two to six eggs. Add seasoning as salt and
pepper or any other to your taste. Add brains to beaten eggs and
scramble in skillet in which butter has been melted. Serve on
toast or with hot biscuits with all sorts of hot sauce or tart jelly.

BOILED VENISON HEART

Clean chambers of the heart well. Cover with water. Add: salt
and pepper, Italian Herb Seasoning, bay leaf. Boil slowly until
tender. Cool 15 minutes before slicing. Heart may be stuffed
with your favorite dressing and served sliced, either hot or
cold.

Nellie Chapin, Michigan

BOILED VENISON TONGUE

Boil tongue in salted, spiced water until tender. Cool in the
water and then peel off the outer layer of skin. Slice and serve
hot or cold with mustard, mayonnaise or horseradish. This is a
marvelous sandwich or salad meat.

VENISON RIBS

Ask your hunter to bring the ribs fresh from the kill and leave as
much meat on them as possible. Parboil the ribs in salted water
to which has been added: Onion and garlic, bay leaf, pickling
spice, salt and pepper. After the ribs are tender but not completely cooked, remove from the water and place in a big roasting pan and dab with your favorite barbecue sauce. Finish
cooking the ribs over the coals of a barbecue pit or in the oven.
This is a rare taste treat.

DOVE

QUAIL &

PHEASANT

DOVE, QUAIL & PHEASANT

Both for sporty shooting and palate-pleasing, we give Number One rank to the Mourning Dove, and his cousin, the Whitewing. Wing shooting of these zippy little birds, especially on a windy day, requires more than average skill.

The dove season also brings back personal memories of autumn in the Haskell country, where a grandfather made it a real privilege for a grandchild to be invited to the grainfields for hunting. The occasion brought spinetingling excitement. The sound of the shotgun . . . the unforgettable aroma of powdery-dry grainstalks . . . children serving as retrievers and birdpickers. (Grandpa Hughes didn't have a dog.)

Dove and football seasons bring a happy blend of recollection. Mrs. Moxley, a kind friend to Texas Tech students at Lubbock, served dove dinners to the youngsters before football games . . . and they carried cold birds in their coatpockets to be eaten at the game.

A Libra coauthor of this book always associates doves with her "special" September birthday dinners. Never did lobster and champagne taste half so good as fried doves, gravy and hot biscuits, with a topping of apple pie.

Dove-cooking is relatively simple if one remembers that game isn't to be prepared like domestic meats. The recipes in this chapter are guaranteed to satisfy even the skeptics about this great delicacy.

While we prefer doves, many others give pheasants or quail first place in the game-cooking scale. Likewise, the quail-shooter prefers this above all forms of the hunting arts. Quail are good eating, almost any way they are cooked.

Likewise with the pheasant, a feast for commoners as well as kings. Even an old pheasant cock can be cooked to mouth-watering perfection.

All game birds should be picked — not skinned. Many hunters will not take the time to pick birds, or have them picked. This is a mistake. While doves and quail can be made into passable fare after skinning, they are much, much better if picked and cooked with the skin intact. Quail are hard to pick without tearing the skin, however.

Picking is much easier if it can be done while the birds are warm. Cleaning can be simplified by using scissors — sometimes called game shears — which are sold widely. After picking, cut along both sides of the bird's backbone. This allows easy removal of head, craw, insides — all in one. Legs and wings can be clipped off easily. A quick washing makes the bird ready for cooking.

Rubber kitchen gloves are good to have along for the dressing operation. Makes things tidier.

FRIED DOVE

Wash and clean the birds carefully, cutting away bloody or bruised flesh. Split down the back, salt, pepper, flour and fry in deep fat.

This is all of the cooking that is necessary if the doves are young. If, however, you have doubts you may want to put the birds in the pressure cooker for a few minutes to insure tenderness.

The gravy in the skillet may need to be enlarged on since the gravy and hot biscuits are an extender for the doves.

Pour off some of the fat in the skillet where the birds were fried. Add the seasoned flour you used to cover the birds originally and when this flour is browned in the skillet, if it seems a little skimpy, add a couple of tablespoons more.

Add water or milk to the browned flour and stir constantly until thickened. Taste for the need of additional salt and pepper. Let us hope you have plenty of doves and only a few people to eat them.

DOVE, QUAIL & PHEASANT

DOVE

Season cleaned dove heavily, mainly with red pepper.

Cover with sliced onion and bay leaf. Marinate in red wine and Worcestershire at least 12 hours. Overnight is better.

Remove dove and pat dry. Brown in fat, preferably butter. Add marinade and bake covered for about an hour. Allow at least two doves for each guest.

Doris Herring, Austin

MOLDED DOVE SALAD

1 cup of cooked dove meat removed from bone
1 envelope of unflavored gelatin
1/4 cup of cold water
1 1/2 cups of hot broth
3 tablespoons of vinegar or lemon juice
1/2 teaspoon of salt
1 chopped hard-boiled egg
1/2 cup chopped celery
1/2 cup of chopped pimiento-stuffed olives

Soften the gelatin in the cold water and dissolve in 1 1/2 cups of hot broth. Allow to cool and in a rinsed salad mold or glass dish arrange olives in the first layer, add some of the gelatin mixture, which has been seasoned with salt and lemon juice. Allow this layer to cool somewhat, then add all of the other ingredients mixed together with the remaining gelatin. Allow to set, and when unmolded serve on a bed of lettuce and top with best quality mayonnaise, preferably homemade. This recipe may be made with other game bird meat.

DOVE PIE

Some hunters (not us) prefer to skin doves and throw away all of the bird except the breast. They freeze these in water in half-gallon cartons, usually an ex-milk container.

Thawing the birds in the water in which they are frozen helps keep in the moisture. When thawed, the birds should be pressure cooked in bouillon until the meat can be picked from the bone. Use 12 to 24 dove breasts and pressure cook about 15 minutes.

In a greased baking dish, large enough to accommodate

DOVE, QUAIL & PHEASANT

your birds, arrange the dove meat. Pour over them a basic white sauce made with:

1 stick of oleo or butter
2 tablespoons of flour
2 cups of broth or sweet milk
  Salt, pepper and a dash of
    Worcestershire sauce

2 hard-boiled eggs, sliced
  Or you may want to add
  mushrooms, English peas
  and carrots.

Cover with pie crust and bake at 350 degrees until the crust is brown. You may prefer to make individual pies.

This bird pie may be made with quail or pheasant or any mixture of these birds.

SACHTLEBEN WILD DOVE CASSEROLE

Pressure cook six wild doves until tender. Remove meat from bone. Chop meat into small pieces and set aside.

Place

3 tablespoons of butter
3 tablespoons of flour in a
    skillet and brown. Add:
3 cups of water and one small
    minced onion

1 small can of mushrooms
  (optional)
1 or two cloves of garlic
  (optional)
  Season to taste with salt and
  pepper

Add chopped dove meat to the above mixture and stir into a baking dish. Cook at a low temperature in the oven for 1 to $1^1/_2$ hours.

Serve over steamed rice or noodles — also good over corn bread. This serves six.

Laura Walser, Blanco

BAKED QUAIL

4 dressed quail
1 cup bread crumbs

Beef stock or bouillon
$^1/_2$ cup shredded almonds

Prepare a stuffing of bread crumbs to which enough beef stock is added to moisten. Mix in almonds and stuff birds. Place in casserole with small amount of water and bake at 325 degrees approximately 40 minutes. Baste often with melted sweet butter. Serve on buttered toast and top with gravy. Serves four.

Francis Raffetto, Dallas

FRIED QUAIL

12 cleaned quail   Flour
    Salt and pepper $^1/_2$ cup of Wesson oil

Cut quail in half — leaving legs together and breast in one piece. Salt, pepper and flour in brown sack, shake quail thoroughly in this mixture. Place in hot Wesson oil in large electric skillet at 400 degrees — browning on both sides. Lower heat to 275 degrees, add one cup of water and simmer for one hour. (These are good to do ahead of time and just simmer until you are ready to eat.)

Remove birds and make milk gravy.
    Serve with hot biscuits.
    Dessert: More biscuits, butter, and homemade fig preserves.
    Should serve twelve.

Ethel Cone, Eagle Lake

BROILED QUAIL OR DOVE

Fresh killed and picked dove and quail are delicious if broiled wrapped in bacon.

           Clean and wash birds.
           Salt and pepper liberally
           Place a pat of butter in the cavity.

Wrap in bacon and place on a rack in your electric skillet or in a casserole in the oven. Broil at 425 degrees until the bacon is crisp. Serve on toast with baked apples or apple sauce.

If the birds are not as tender as you would like when the bacon has crisped, add a little moisture as one-half cup of water or white wine and steam for a few minutes at a 350 degree heat.

QUAIL WITH GREEN GRAPES

4 quail
Salt, pepper, flour
1 stick of butter
$^1/_2$ cup water
$^1/_2$ cup seedless green grapes

2 tablespoons chopped
  pecans
1 tablespoon lemon juice
4 buttered toast slices

Sprinkle quail inside and out with salt, pepper and flour. Melt butter in skillet; add quail and brown on all sides. Add water, cover and cook until tender. Stir in nuts, lemon juice and grapes.

Serve quail on buttered toast slices with sauce in pan, wild rice, and whole baked tomatoes stuffed with peas. Serves four.

FRIED QUAIL

Tom Waddell of Eagle Lake, one of America's great outdoorsmen, used the following recipe for frying quail:

Pick the birds (don't skin them). Split each quail in half. Salt and pepper. Then put in refrigerator to season for two hours. Sprinkle with flour or dip in batter. Cook in deep fryer . . . cooking oil smoking. Eight to ten halves can be cooked at a time, and the birds will come out tender and succulent.

MARINATED QUAIL

20 quail (prefers them skinned
     and split down the back)
3 tablespoons brown sugar
2 cans beef bouillon
2 teaspoon oregano

1 clove garlic, well minced
$^1/_2$ cup good oil
$^1/_2$ cup soy sauce
$^1/_2$ cup rose wine
1 cup white port

Mix dry ingredients first. Pepper birds all over. Mix ingredients together and pour over birds. Marinate three- and one-half hours. Cook in covered pot at 375 degrees for one- and one-half hours. Do NOT salt. Bouillon has plenty.

Judge Ross E. Doughty, Uvalde

ROAST PHEASANT

Squeeze the juice of one lemon on each pheasant to be cooked, both inside and out. Allow to stand for 30 minutes or more. Salt and pepper the birds and dot with butter. Wrap the birds in strips of bacon and place in an open roaster or casserole to cook at 350 degrees about an hour. Remove birds and use the drippings for gravy, adding wine, mushrooms or several tablespoons of tart jelly. Spoon this over the pheasant and serve on toast.

CHUKAR
(Also called Rock Partridge.
Imported from Eastern Europe and Asia)

FRIED CHUKAR

Parboil the birds in bouillon for 20 minutes. Remove from liquid. Season. Flour . . . Fry rapidly in hot fat. Serve with gravy and hot biscuits.

PRESSURE COOKED

If you have doubt about the age or tenderness of the birds, apply lemon juice, salt and pepper to them, and brown in fat in a pressure cooker. Remove and set aside the birds. Pour off fat. Return birds to pressure cooker. Add one can of bouillon and pressure cook for 10 minutes. Add a splash of wine after cooking. Serve on rice or toast.

BROILED

Young, tender birds are tastiest when sprinkled with lemon juice and allowed to rest for 20 minutes before salting, peppering and dotting with butter (or covering with strips of bacon).

DOVE, QUAIL & PHEASANT

Broil 15 to 20 minutes, basting with butter and lemon juice to keep from becoming dry.

(Note: Chukars are game birds with very little natural fat. Fat and moisture must be added for proper cooking.)

DOVE, QUAIL & PHEASANT

TURKEY

That grand old American native, the wild turkey, which some pioneers contended (properly, we think) should have been our national symbol, thrives in Texas and other parts of the United States.

Once wild turkeys became so depleted that few cooks ever had occasion to prepare one. But the big birds are being bagged by the thousands during the present fall hunting season, and by the hundreds in the Texas spring gobbler season.

Just as venison should never be compared with beef for cooking, never look upon wild turkey as one does the broadbreasted domestic turkey. The big birds look a lot alike and even interbreed. But otherwise the comparison is about like a milkcow and a racehorse.

The wild turkey is structured for running and flying. His tendons are too tough to be cut with an ordinary knife.

Yet the turkey properly prepared is delicious. The ranchcountry citizen usually skins a wild turkey for convenience. While ordinarily we favor picking game birds over skinning them, an exception is in order for the turkey. It is seldom convenient to pluck the feathers soon after the bird is killed. Picking a cold bird is a real task and too much to expect of a weary hunter at the end of the day. Furthermore, few commercial locker plants will accept a feathered bird for processing, and those providing pickers charge enormous prices (we don't blame them).

The turkey's craw and insides should be removed immediately after it is killed, and the bird hung in the open air, preferably a screened porch. The skinning can be performed easily at any time. Keep the beard and/or leg shank showing spurs on the turkey until you get home, otherwise you might hve a problem with the game warden.

Gobblers are legal almost everywhere during the season, and hens increasingly are being legalized as game in Texas. The hen is better eating, more tender. The hen also is much smaller. Yearling gobblers, which stay with the hens during the first winter while the older gobblers take to the hills, also are very good eating.

A baked turkey must be picked.

The easiest thing to do with a wild turkey is skin off the feathers as soon as the hunter gets home, and cut up the bird for future cooking, throwing away the carcass. This involves removing the breast meat in two large slabs by cutting along the flat center bone.

Legs should be removed first. The first and second joints can be boiled later until the meat separates from the bone, which solves the problem of tough tendons. The meat can be removed with fingers, and it makes fine eating for almost any dish calling for poultry.

The breast can be cooked in various ways, including sliced and fried as camp cooks usually do it.

As with all birds and animals, the flavor and quality of turkey meat depends on the age of the bird and what it has been eating. Cooks therefore should cheer the hunter who brings home a hen bagged while eating corn. These taste better than the old trophy gobblers who "step on their beards" in the high country and dine on cedar berries.

Credible witnesses report a phenomenon of wild turkey. At certain seasons in South Texas, turkeys fill up on chilipequins, the tiny hot peppers eaten with meals by so many Texans in the brush country. Chilipequin grow wild over much of Texas, beginning as tiny green peppers, they later turn fiery red to match their flavor.

When wild turkeys feast on chilipequin, and are soon after bagged by hunters, flesh becomes pre-peppered, sometimes too hot for the taste of an outlander. At least, that's how the natives tell it.

The tastiest "turkey" we ever ate turned out to be a female

peacock, running with a flock of turkeys in the hill country. The bird was shot as a curiosity. A Mexican camp cook fried the breast, which came out like the finest pheasant, only larger.

BAKED WILD TURKEY

Hopefully your wild turkey has been shot in the head. If there are bruised or bloody places in the meat, trim it away. Soak turkey in water to which one-half cup of vinegar has been added.

A wild turkey reminds one of a basketball player — mostly legs. It is sometimes difficult to fit the bird in an ordinary roaster, so wrapping in foil is a good solution.

Dry the bird and season inside and out with salt and pepper. Stuff the bird with bread dressing if desired. If not, fill the cavity with chopped onion, celery and tart apple. Butter the bird generously and wrap in foil. Cook at least 3–4 hours at 325 degrees. When you open the foil to test for doneness, add more butter and if you wish to brown the bird leave the foil open, turn up the oven to broil until the bird is ready for the table.

Serve with a molded red salad, sweet potatoes and broccoli.

Happy Thanksgiving.

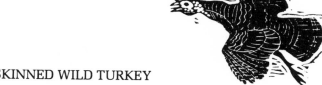

SKINNED WILD TURKEY

Since it is increasingly difficult to get a wild turkey picked commercially, skinning seems to be the best alternative.

Cut the breast and legs away from the back. The back may be boiled for the broth or to make soup or gravy.

The breast may be baked over dressing or chopped vegetables, buttered well and wrapped in foil. This is a very dry meat, so basting from time to time is necessary. Wrapping the breast in bacon or adding larding fat helps keep the meat moist.

The breast may also be pressure cooked and used in molded meat salads, spaghetti or turkey salad. The legs and thighs, pressure cooked and removed from the bone, may also be used where any cooked fowl is recommended.

TURKEY

WILD TURKEY IN A T-SHIRT

1 skinned wild turkey
1 old clean T-shirt
1 stick of butter, oleo or bacon
   drippings

1 chopped onion
2 ribs of chopped celery
  Salt and pepper

Imagine our distress when we found our Thanksgiving wild turkey, brought home from the locker plant still wrapped, had been skinned rather than picked.

The only thing we had to wrap the bare bird in was a clean old T-shirt.

The bird was salted, peppered and stuffed with the chopped onion and celery. The T-shirt was dampened and dipped in melted butter. We clothed the turkey in the T-shirt and cooked it in a 325 degree oven for two and a half hours. It was the best wild turkey ever.

WILD TURKEY SALAD

2 cups of coarsely chopped
   cooked wild turkey
1 cup of chopped celery

2 hard-boiled eggs, chopped
  Homemade mayonnaise to
   moisten

Mix all together and season with salt and pepper if needed. Serve in lettuce cups with sweet pickles and sliced tomatoes. This should serve four or more.

WILD TURKEY CURRY

2 cups of coarsely chopped
   and boned wild turkey
1 cup of chopped celery
1 cup of chopped apple

$3/4$ cup of mayonnaise
$1/2$ teaspoon of curry powder
$1/8$ teaspoon of ginger

Mold in one package of unflavored gelatin. Serve on lettuce leaf with mayonnaise and any other salad garnishes as sliced tomato, cucumber, avocado, asparagus, sliced hard-boiled egg, and potato chips.

TURKEY

BARBECUED WILD TURKEY

2 sticks of butter or oleo
1 No. 2 can of tomato paste
1 bottle of catsup
$^1/_2$ cup of vinegar
2 tablespoons of sugar
6 teaspoons paprika
1 onion, grated
1 clove of garlic, mashed
4 teaspoon of salt

4 teaspoon of chili powder
3 teaspoon Worcestershire
   sauce
2 teaspoon black pepper
$^1/_2$ teaspoon Tabasco Sauce
   Juice of 1 lemon (and
      include some of the rind)
2 cans of beer

Wash and dry the cleaned, whole turkey. Season inside and out with salt and pepper. Loosen outside skin with handle of long spoon and squirt the barbecue mixture inside of skin.

Rub outside of turkey with butter and place in roaster with a rack. Cover with the barbecue sauce, using beer. Cover or wrap in foil and bake. Baste from time to time during roasting period. Cook at about 300 degrees for several hours.

WILD TURKEY SPAGHETTI

This full recipe is enough to feed an army. As a matter of fact, our daughter gave this recipe to a Mess Sergeant in Germany, and it was served to the troops in the field. Vary the amounts depending on the quantity of meat.

2 packages of spaghetti
4–5 cups of cooked turkey
3 cans of mushrooms (stems
   and pieces or buttons if
   fancy)
2 large onions
1 pound of butter or substitute

1 small clove of garlic or $^1/_4$
   teaspoon garlic powder
2 bunches of celery
2 large green peppers
3 large cans of tomatoes
1 pound of grated cheese
   Salt, pepper and chopped
      parsley

Melt butter in large skillet or Dutch oven, sauté onions but do not burn. Add tomatoes, garlic, peppers and parsley and cook slowly for 2 hours. Add chopped celery and mushrooms and cook until tender. Season to taste.

Add cooked turkey and 1 cup of broth and simmer for 30 minutes. Have spaghetti cooked and blanched. Pour sauce over all and add grated cheese. Leave this to warm until cheese is melted.

TURKEY

This freezes well, and is really tastier the second day. Leftovers can be frozen in an oven bag and dropped in hot water to thaw and heat.

WILD TURKEY TITTIES

Skin and slice the breast of the wild turkey. The slices should be finger length and about one-fourth inch thick.

Soak the slices in milk for one-half to one hour.

Salt, pepper and flour and cook in hot fat until brown. Remove and drain.

Pour off excess fat. Stir in one tablespoon of flour for each cup of milk to make gravy. Brown the flour in the fat and slowly add the milk that the turkey has been soaked in. Stir constantly. When thickened taste for seasoning.

Serve Titties with hot biscuits, gravy and honey.

This recipe can be prepared in camp or at home.

Cindy Nix, Austin

WILD TURKEY AND NOODLE ALMONDINE CASSEROLE

2 eight ounce packages of noodles	Meat from legs, thighs, wings of wild turkey pressure cooked for 20 minutes.
2 cans of cream of mushroom soup	
2 small cans of mushrooms (button)	$1/_2$ can of white wine

Cook noodles in boiling, salted water for 6 minutes. Drain.

Dilute cream of mushroom soup with $1/_2$ can of white wine and juice from canned mushrooms. Heat with boned and chopped turkey. Mix with cooked noodles and fill large, flat, greased baking dish with the mix.

Cover with slivered almonds and bake in a 350 degree oven until the dish is bubbly and heated through.

This is a great dish for the Christmas buffet or the PTA supper.

TURKEY

WILD TURKEY SOUP

Simmer turkey carcass in water to cover, with onion, salt and celery until done. Remove skin and bones, then add small white beans, meat and 1 tablespoon of Rosemary to liquid. Simmer gently until beans are tender.

Serve in large bowls with corn bread and a green salad.

Eleanor Halbert Nichols, Plainview

JAVELINA, SQUIRREL & 'POSSUM

An increasing game animal of the Southwest is the javelina, a fierce-looking beast found frequently in deer-hunting country. Javelinas, technically the Collared Peccary, usually run in herds, and tales abound about whether these animals are truly ferocious or just have a frightening appearance — with their long tusks and bristles up.

The javelina makes a good conversation piece. They are rather social outcasts, both among other denizens of the wild and in hunting camps. This is partly because the pig-looking animal is noisy, and deer like it quiet. A band of javelinas also eats up the food supply quickly.

Most anti-social, however, is the javelina's odor. It has a musk gland along the backbone just forward of the tail. While all wild game have musk glands, the javelina overdoes it.

Properly dressed and cooked, the javelina makes good eating. Many Mexican-Americans in the brush country lay in javelinas for winter eating like Southerners kill and lay in hogs. These javelina aficionados usually remove the long muscles of the hindquarters, throw away the "white parts" of gristle and bone, and cook the remainder almost like backstrap. Guests in our home — including some who have known javelinas for years without eating any — have been astonished to learn that the tasty meat they ate came from the animal that is incorrectly called a wild hog. Our area has wild hogs too, including big Russian boars, but that isn't in our cookbook.

Dressing and cooking a javelina isn't for everyone, but it is worth the effort.

Since the hunter often has a choice of targets in a javelina herd, he should select a young sow or even a pig for a target. The bigger boar makes a more formidable wall trophy but he's hard to convert into any meat dish other than chili.

The musk gland — worn by both sexes — needs to be removed in the field dressing, and it's handy to have those rubberized gloves along for this operation. Then the javelina should be aired and skinned as soon as possible. The hide remains antisocial for quite a while, but it does make the very finest gloves we have ever owned.

Javelina skin is light and very durable, and tans into a beautiful pearl white finish. Your taxidermist can handle the hide and tell you where to get gloves manufactured. Two pairs of gloves can be made from one hide, unless the head is mounted. In this case, only enough hide remains for a single pair of gloves. The javelina, as this illustrates, is about half head and neck, which may account partly for his fierce appearance and relatively small amount of edible meat.

JAVELINA

Thaw frozen meat in water with 2 tablespoons of vinegar added.

Pat the meat dry and squeeze the juice of 1 or 2 lemons on all sides of the meat. Salt and pepper.

Wrap in foil and bake one hour at 350 degrees.

Open foil and apply barbecue sauce — cook another hour or so uncovered, basting with sauce from time to time.

JAVELINA BARBECUE SAUCE

1 stick oleo or butter
2 tablespoons chopped onion

Juice and rind of 1 lemon
1 cup of water

Simmer the above together for 10 minutes. Add:

1/2 bottle of catsup
4 tablespoons Worcestershire sauce
2 tablespoons of prepared mustard

Garlic sauce if desired
Hot sauce if desired
Salt and pepper

FRIED SQUIRREL

Rinse skinned squirrel in cold water and pat dry. dip in buttermilk and then in seasoned flour and fry in hot fat just as you would a chicken.

If the squirrel is young, you probably will not need to steam the meat. If there is any doubt, drain off excess fat in the skillet, add about a cup of water or wine if you prefer, and steam covered for about 15 minutes. Or you may wish to pressure cook the meat for an additional 5 to 10 minutes.

Make gravy in the frying fat by adding the leftover seasoned flour and milk or water. Serve over rice or with hot biscuits.

SQUIRREL STEW

Cleaned and skinned squirrel cut in serving size pieces

4 ribs of celery, cut diagonally
Small whole onions
Small whole potatoes
4 carrots, sliced diagonally

1 small bay leaf
Salt, pepper and
Worcestershire to taste

Place squirrel pieces in Dutch oven or heavy skillet with a lid. Cover with water and steam until the meat is nearly tender. Add the vegetables and seasoning and cook until just tender.

If a thickened gravy is desired, add 1 tablespoon of corn starch dissolved in one-half cup of water just before serving.

This is good served with corn bread.

One squirrel will serve two or three people.

JAVELINA, SQUIRREL & POSSUM

'POSSUM (Opossum)
(Army Cooking, 1910 Style, from an old U.S. Army manual.)

Clean and skin the 'possums, allowing them to hang in the open air for several hours, then place in refrigerator for at least 24 hours before cooking. Stuff with an ordinary bread stuffing (sage preferred).

Set in a deep pan so that no part will project above the top; season well with pepper and salt, and pour about one inch of beef stock or canned beef bouillon into the pan.

Fill the vacant spaces with peeled sweet potatoes, and sprinkle a little flour over the whole; cover with a crust, the same for a pot pie, omitting the fat, as the crust will be removed after baking and will not be served.

Allow to bake slowly for about three hours. Remove crust and serve hot. The crust will absorb most of the fat from the opossum.

LYNETTE'S 'POSSUM

Dress and skin the 'possum. Remove as much fat as possible from outside of carcass and be especially careful to remove any glandular tissue from hind legs.

Salt and pepper 'possum well, then place in oven bag and cover with thick slices of onion. Close bag and punch holes in top as directed. Cook in a very slow oven 225 degrees about 45 minutes per pound. Meat falls off the bone with this treatment and is delicious.

JAVELINA, SQUIRREL & POSSUM

DUCKS & GEESE

Government regulations have made waterfowl shooting almost too complicated for mere mortals, but it is worth a trip to the Lissie Prairie near Eagle Lake, just to see and hear the giant flocks that come down from Canada each fall to help harvest the rice crop.

This is the best time to take ducks and geese — while they are fat on rice or other grain.

The hunter usually takes what he can get among these high flying birds, within the limits of the government's point system, which requires the hunter to have the eyes and know-how of a game biologist to avoid breaking the law accidentally by bagging the wrong variety.

Fortunately, the system favors taking the magnificent pintail drake (sprig), one of the largest and best-tasting ducks. Teal (which have a special season) are regarded by some as being a bit finer fare. All ducks are good if properly cooked (possibly excepting the so-called bottom feeders which live on fish and other marine growth).

Geese are grand birds. The Specklebelly (Whitefront) is universally regarded as the best eating, and it is one of the most highly-protected by law. Another "dark" goose, the Blue, probably is next to the Speck as table fare, followed by Canadas (Ringneck) and the frequently more abundant Snow Goose.

Young Snows, which are gray-colored on their first trips South, make especially fine eating.

Picking of ducks and geese is most essential if you want good eating. In most areas where waterfowl hunting is extensive, commercial picking plants are available. A newly-killed bird can be handpicked fairly rapidly but we recommend the commercial places where available. They use hot water for picking. One suggestion is to make sure you get back from the picking plant the birds that you leave there. Mix-ups are common. Also, if you want the giblets (we don't particularly care for them), tell the picker when you leave the birds; otherwise, you are out of luck.

While ducks and geese usually are picked and cleaned about like chickens, small ducks lend themselves well to being split up the back with knife or game shears. This is a good way to clean them, and improves the carcass for cooking.

BAKED WILD DUCK

For each guest prepare one duck if small, $^1/_2$ if large.
   Season heavily with red pepper and salt.
   Place onion in cavity, also celery and apple, if desired.
   Brown each duck in deep, hot bacon grease, turning from side to side until the skin looks like it will pop.
   Earlier, brown a cup of flour or more in the oven until it is cinnamon color, smoothing with the back-side of a spoon so that it will brown evenly. This is a slow process and can be done days in advance and stored in the refrigerator.
   Mix flour in bacon grease with water to make a thin gravy. You may need to pour off some of the excess fat, but you need enough gravy in the roaster to cover the breast of the ducks. Add coffee (black and strong) and Worcestershire to season.
   Place ducks breast down in gravy and cook slowly at 350 degrees until tender. This will take an hour or more.

Doris Herring, Austin

Doris Herring probably served wild ducks to more guests than anyone in Austin. Asked why she used only red pepper as seasoning, she replied that her grandfather felt black pepper was very unhealthy but that red pepper was acceptable. She also believed, like other good game cooks, that game should be well done and cooked moist.

BAKED DUCK

6 Teal ducks	Salt and pepper
6 onion pieces	2 tablespoons Wesson Oil
6 celery pieces	1 cup Sherry cooking wine

Rub ducks thoroughly with salt and pepper — place onion and celery pieces in cavity.

Heat 2 tablespoons of oil in a flat baking dish and roll ducks in hot oil finally resting them breast-side up. Pour in one cup of wine and cover, sealing tightly with aluminum foil. Bake one hour at 350 degrees. This same method of cooking may be used with larger ducks. Should serve six.

Ethel Cone, Eagle Lake

WILD DUCK — SPANISH

For each duck use:

1 clove garlic	$1/_2$ bottle of catsup
Chopped onion and celery	$1/_4$ cup of water
$1/_2$ bottle of Lea and Perrins	
Worcestershire Sauce	

For the entire batch, add one chopped green pepper and all giblets.

In the cavity of each duck, place garlic, onion and celery. Cover breast with salt and black pepper.

Place in roaster, cover with sauce and bake covered at 375 degrees until tender. More water may need to be added from time to time.

For gravy, thicken the sauce left in the roaster with flour and serve with rice.

Pat Crockett

DUCK WITH CHILI DRESSING

Use any duck

$1/_4$ loaf of day-old bread	1 bay leaf
4 corn muffins	2 cups of water
3 ribs of celery	$1/_4$ pound of butter
1 onion	

Boil the celery, onion and bay leaf in the water until slightly tender. Add the butter and pour over the crumbled bread crumbs. Season with salt, pepper and 2 tablespoons of chili powder.

Use this dressing to stuff ducks. Any leftover dressing can be placed in the bottom of the roaster. Place ducks breast down in the dressing.

Cook in a 550-degree oven for 20 minutes uncovered. Turn heat to 350 degrees, cover and cook until tender which will take about two hours.

RUDDY DUCK

One young ruduck duck   Juice of one lemon
Bread stuffing or commercial   1 stick of butter
   mix

Split the duck down the back. Salt, pepper and squeeze the juice of the lemon inside and out.

Place the duck over the moistened bread stuffing in a casserole breast up. Butter the breast generously and bake covered about one hour. Baste from time to time with butter.

One duck will serve two people and this particular variety is the most delicious we have ever tasted.

DUCKS AND GEESE IN CASSEROLE

4 geese or 8 ducks or a $^1/_2$ cup of Madeira wine
   combination   Chopped white onions,
6 or 8 slices of bacon   chopped carrots and
   Salt   celery
   Cayenne pepper   Chopped garlic to taste —
1 can of orange juice   up to three cloves
   concentrate — 1 can of
   water

Use only the skinned breast of the geese and skinned ducks cut into serving pieces.

In a heavy iron skillet cook the bacon slices until almost done. Remove the bacon and set aside. Dust the meat with cayenne pepper and sauté in the bacon fat until lightly browned.

Remove meat from the skillet and place breast down in a deep casserole. Cover with orange juice, water, wine and the chopped vegetables. Cook at 250 degrees F for two and a half hours. Remove the pot vegetables and discard. Taste for salt and pepper. Remove meat from the bones and serve over white or brown rice. Broiled tomatoes and red wine make good compliments for a game dinner.

This recipe can be prepared in either the CROCK-POT or the CLAY POT.

John F. Morehead, Austin

ORANGE SAUCE FOR WATERFOWL

1 whole orange   ¹/₂ cup of sugar
1 stick of butter

Section one whole orange, rind and all, and grind very fine. In a sauce pan melt one stick of butter. Add ¹/₂ cup of sugar and the ground orange. Heat all together and serve warm over ducks or geese. If this sauce is too sweet for your taste add lemon juice to obtain the right tartness.

Sliced oranges over ducks while they are cooking seems to complement them.

FRIED DUCK

3 or 4 large wild ducks   Salt, pepper and flour
2 tablespoon salt   Wesson oil
³/₄ cup vinegar

Cut wings and legs off and slice meat in large chunks from the breast. Soak cut-up pieces approximately one hour in warm water, salt and vinegar. Drain well. Sprinkle with salt, pepper and flour. Fry in deep fat slowly. Do not overcook.

This is good served with Pepper Jelly.

Should serve six.

Ethel Cone, Eagle Lake

ROAST WILD GOOSE

1 wild goose (hopefully young)	Salt and pepper
Lemon or orange juice	Sliced bacon or chunks of fat
1 stick of butter	boiling bacon

If the goose is frozen, thaw in water to which 2 tablespoons of vinegar have been added. Pat dry and generously squeeze lemon or orange juice inside and out. Season with salt and pepper and cover the breast with strips of bacon or add chunks of fat meat inside, over breast, at wings and leg juncture to the body.

Cover tightly or wrap in foil and bake slowly at 325 degrees until tender, about 2 hours. Baste with butter if necessary.

If you like, place thinly sliced oranges over the bacon on the breast and inside the bird.

Lemon, orange, apple and apricot flavors enhance the goose. Dressings may be made and fruit-flavored. Or the goose can be served with baked apples, apple sauce, sweet and sour sauce or with rice cooked with orange peel and juice.

FROZEN GOOSE

Place frozen goose in a covered container with:

1 can of bouillon	Celery tops and outside
2 cans of water	stalks
1 bay leaf	6 whole cloves
1 onion	1 clove of garlic

Steam for three hours. Remove to oven and brown.

Goose can be served with kraut relish or any of the cabbage-type vegetables, such as brussel sprouts or broccoli.

GOOSE SAUCE — SWEET AND SOUR

$1/_4$ cup of tart jelly (Guava,	2 tablespoons Sherry
Mustang Grape, Grape,	Salt and pepper to taste
Plum or Wild Berry)	Lemon juice until sour
3 tablespoons of butter.	

Warm this together and serve over ducks or geese.

DUCKS & GEESE

SWEET AND SOUR SAUCE FOR VENISON OR DUCK

Brown in

2 tablespoons of oleo or butter:	Add mixed separately
3 green onions	$^3/_4$ cup chicken or beef bouillon
$^1/_2$ green pepper	$^1/_2$ cup sugar
$^1/_2$ red pepper	$^1/_2$ cup vinegar
3 stalks of celery	$2^1/_2$ tablespoons corn starch
	2 tablespoons soy sauce

If venison is raw, cut in chunks and brown with the vegetables listed above. If cooked, add to total sauce plus 1 can of bean sprouts and heat thoroughly.

To serve over ducks simply cut baked duck into serving pieces and cover with sauce.

Cooked rice or chow mein noodles are a good base for venison or duck with sauce.

WILD GOOSE WITH SAUERKRAUT

1 cleaned wild goose	Bacon drippings
1 quart of sauerkraut	Salt and pepper to taste

Open two large cans of kraut and heat in large skillet with one-half cup of bacon drippings. Stuff goose with the hot kraut mixture and place in covered roaster. Any remaining kraut and juice can be placed in the bottom of the roaster and used to baste the fowl while cooking.

Roast at 325 degrees until tender, an hour or more. Test for doneness by pulling a wing away from the body. Do not puncture skin on the breast.

You may or may not wish to eat the sauerkraut when the goose is done. If not, serve the bird with cabbage-type vegetables, such as turnips, brussel sprouts or broccoli.

GOOSE LIVER PATE

This may also be made of duck livers, and the amount increased by adding chicken livers.

Place in a sauce pan washed livers, salt, chopped onion,

and celery salt. Boil until tender, then press through a sieve. Add enough brandy to moisten.

At serving time, combine this mixture with melted butter or mayonnaise to spread on crackers or thin dry toast.

WATERFOWL STEW

1 goose or duck cut into serving-size pieces	1 or 2 whole onions
1 can of beef bouillon	1 to 1½ cups of sliced celery (cut in chunks)
4 cups of water	Peppercorns and salt to taste
1 bay leaf	

Wash the waterfowl and place in covered pot or Dutch oven with all of the ingredients above and simmer slowly until tender. Add cooked carrots, potatoes, green peas or whatever stew vegetables you have in the house. The canned mixed vegetables are good or the frozen ones.

Add one-half cup of good red wine and serve. If the stock needs thickening, add 2 tablespoons of corn starch dissolved in one-half cup of water.

This recipe can serve a few or many depending on how much waterfowl you have to cook and how many vegetables you wish to add. Be sure you have at least one potato for each guest and a whole carrot.

GUMBO

3 tablespoons butter or margarine	2 wild ducks, cut in frying pieces
3 tablespoons of flour	Green onion tops, chopped
1 large onion chopped	About 10 ounces of chopped okra
1 green pepper chopped	Filé
1 cup of celery chopped	Dash of Worcestershire
1 small pod of garlic	Dash or two of Tabasco

In a large iron pot or skillet, melt the butter or margarine at a low temperature, stir in the flour, stirring constantly,, until a rich brown color. (You have made a roux.) Add the chopped vegetables, then four quarts of water and salt and pepper to taste.

Meanwhile skin the ducks, boil briefly in water or beef bouillon. Remove from the water, salt, pepper, flour and brown in hot fat. When browned add the ducks to the vegetable liquid and cook until tender. Cook the liquid down by one third. This may take two or three hours. Just before serving add the onion tops and filé.

If desired add two cans of crab meat.

Do not boil after filé has been added. Let rest for 48 hours or more and serve hot over rice.

If you precook the ducks, the water or bouillon may be used to make up the 4 quarts of liquid.

Any leftover rice may be added to the gumbo pot.

Serves ten.

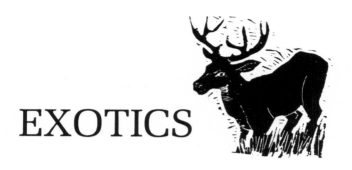

EXOTICS

An important and growing source of game shooting and cooking is the "exotic" — a name applied to all foreign game animals.

Numerous varieties of deer, antelope, wild sheep and hogs transplanted from other lands are found to thrive in Texas. The animals are brought here mostly by commercial game ranches, and are exempt from the hunting restrictions imposed on native game. The hunter is charged by the landowner for what he kills.

Many recipes already given in this book can be used for foreign game. Below are a couple tried specifically on exotics in our kitchen and found to be good.

MOUFLON SHEEP

4–5 pound Mouflon roast, shoulder or ham, thawed in water to which 2 tablespoons of vinegar has been added. Remove roast, pat dry and place in roaster in the oven at 425 degrees. Cook uncovered until the roast has seared, about 30–40 minutes. Lower the heat to 350 degrees and continue cooking, uncovered, for 3–4 hours and baste frequently with the following sauce:

In a sauce pan heat together:

1 stick of butter or oleo
1 bottle of Worcestershire
    sauce
$^1/_2$ cup of water
    Juice of two lemons and
      rind of $^1/_2$ lemon
2 tablespoons of vinegar

2 tablespoons of prepared
    mustard
1 medium onion, grated
2 tablespoons of sugar
2 teaspoons of salt
$^1/_2$ teaspoon of pepper

Serve as you would a leg of lamb with small boiled onions, English peas and mint jelly. Serves six to eight.

SIKA DEER

1 pound of deer chops or round
  Buttermilk
  Flour, salt and pepper

Thaw deer in buttermilk. Dip in seasoned flour and brown in fat in a pressure cooker. Remove meat and pour off excess fat. Use seasoned flour in pressure cooker to make a quart of thin gravy. Taste for more salt and pepper. Return deer to gravy and pressure cook for 15 minutes.

    Remove to hot platter and serve with rice and deer gravy. This should serve four.

ARMADILLO

This prehistoric animal is seldom killed for the dinner table, but the Armadillo has its following. Citizens of Victoria, Texas, annually hold an Armadillo Festival which features championships both for Armadillo racing and Armadillo cooking.

Long before city folk discovered the Armadillo as a sporting beast and table delicacy, many rural residents knew the secret of Armadillo cookery.

While we have never learned to distinguish between sexes of Armadillos, especially in the dim light of dawn or late evening when humans most often see them, a young animal is the best to eat. This means usually a less than full-grown Armadillo, if you can find one. The Armadillo digs for food, worms and roots mostly, and is a garden predator, generally considered a pest.

Clean an Armadillo by splitting up the underside and removing the innards. Carve the carcass out of the shell, leaving a delicate clean meat.

Traditional Armadillo cooking resembles the style of how Hawaiians prepare pigs at a luau.

This calls for digging a hole deep and large enough to hold the Armadillo after being lined with foil (or if you are a real primitive, large leaves). The cooking pit will be covered with a metal lid, such as corrugated iron left over from your tin roof.

Armadillo eaters are leisurely people. Be prepared for a 24-hour wait while dinner is being cooked. This is done by keeping hot coals on the metal hole cover. When cooked in its own juice, the Armadillo is succulent, although other recipes call for sauces.

Armadillo also is said to be tasty when cut up and fried like chicken. This way, you don't need 24 hours for cooking the main course.

Below are two recipes recommended by Victoria residents in championship competition:

ARMADILLO BARBECUE

Armadillo is very much like pork and can be cooked in the same way. Texans especially appreciate it barbecued, and following is a recipe for barbecue mop (which is used over the meat while cooking) and the barbecue sauce served with the meal when done.

BARBECUE MOP

2 cups of cooking oil	2 tablespoons of Worcestershire sauce
$1/_2$ cup of vinegar	$1/_2$ teaspoon of salt
1 onion chopped	$1/_4$ teaspoon of black pepper
1 lemon sliced thin	$1/_2$ teaspoon of garlic powder

Mix all ingredients in sauce pan and cook 10 minutes at medium heat. Brush meat while cooking.

Emily Buckert, Victoria

BARBECUE SAUCE

1 stick of butter or margarine	1 tablespoon of prepared mustard
1 bottle of catsup	1 tablespoon of Worcestershire Sauce
$1/_2$ onion finely chopped	Salt and pepper
Juice of one lemon	$1/_4$ teaspoon of garlic powder

Mix all ingredients together and simmer for 10 minutes. If you prefer a thinner sauce add $1/_2$ can of beef bouillon.

Serve with cooked meat.

ARMADILLO

ARMADILLO STUFFED WITH SWEET POTATO COMPOTE

Boil and mash four sweet potatoes.
Dice one onion and two ribs of celery.
Add to mashed potatoes:

2 tablespoons of brown sugar	$1/_4$ teaspoon of pepper
3 dashes of cinnamon	3 dashes of Tabasco
$1/_2$ teaspoon of salt	

Roll Armadillo carcass in flour and cornmeal mixture. Stuff with sweet potato compote. Place in a three-inch deep baking pan and bake for three hours at 285 degrees. Baste during cooking with two cups of white wine to which two tablespoons of olive oil have been added.

Fred Armstrong Victoria

SIDE DISHES

SIDE DISHES

Just as game cooking can be plain or fancy, side dishes range from simple to gourmet.

Our experience on hunting trips, where food generally is plain and fattening, includes unusual (for us) bread. Hunters regularly stock up on the "homemade" bread and pastries of Fredericksburg bakeries.

At a ranch near Athens we enjoyed good tasting sour dough biscuits of the simplest recipe. This consisted of pouring beer (ours was flat left overnight in a near-empty barrel) into a commercial biscuit mix, working the dough into the right consistency, and dropping the biscuits into a pan for baking.

A highlight of any visit to the Dolph Briscoe Ranch near Catarina, is predawn breakfast with the Mexican cowboys in the cookhouse, where thick tortillas are made in iron skillets and kept warm — stacked in heated dishpans lined with clean dishtowels. The diner just breaks off the quantity of bread he wants.

BASIC STUFFING RECIPES FOR GAME

One quart of dried bread crumbs. (Use day-old bread, cold biscuits or left-over cornbread.) One quart will stuff one duck.

1 stick of butter or oleo	Salt, pepper and poultry
1/2 cup of chopped onion	season to taste
1/2 cup of chopped celery	2 whole eggs
	Hot water or giblet broth to
	moisten

Melt the fat in a skillet and lightly brown the onions. Add all ingredients to bread crumbs and mix well. Add enough moisture to make dressing of your desired consistency.

Some prefer a dry dressing so very little liquid is necessary.

Stuff bird very lightly with dressing before baking, or place the dressing in a separate casserole and serve with gravy as an extra dish.

APPLE STUFFING: Use the above basic recipe and add $1\frac{1}{2}$ cups of chopped apple.

APRICOT STUFFING: Add $1\frac{1}{2}$ cups of dried apricots to the basic recipe.

OYSTER STUFFING: Add one-half pint of fresh oysters to the basic recipe.

SAUSAGE STUFFING: Add one-half pound of pork sausage which has been cooled and crumbled into the basic recipe.

CHESTNUT OR PECAN STUFFING: Add one cup of fresh boiled chestnuts to the basic recipe or 1 cup of Texas pecans.

WILD RICE DRESSING

Cook $1\frac{1}{2}$ cups of wild rice according to directions. Bake one recipe of cornbread in advance. Dressing:
Lightly sauté in $\frac{1}{4}$ pound of butter:

> 1 large onion, finely minced
> 1 cup of celery, chopped

Add 2 large cans of stems and pieces of mushrooms (drained). Salt, pepper and savory salt to taste.

Crumble cornbread, add wild rice, any giblets and about $\frac{2}{3}$ cup of broth and sautéed vegetables. Mix well. Taste for need of additional salt and pepper.
Add:

> 1 large crumbled bay leaf
> 1 tablespoon chili powder
> Savory salt

SIDE DISHES

Mix well and if a bird is to be stuffed, use a small amount for that purpose. The remainder goes in a buttered casserole, and if possible, chill a few hours in the refrigerator. Let dressing be very moist. Add a tablespoon of Vermouth just before starting to bake. (Optional)

Cook covered the first 45 minutes, then uncovered 15 minutes in a 350 degree oven.

Note: Half wild rice and half white rice may be substituted in this recipe. (Cooked separately, of course.) Just the rice, vegetables, mushrooms, plus salt, pepper and savory salt makes a delicious dish served with game if you don't want to go all the way to dressing.

Judith Chapin, Lampasas

RICE DRESSING

1 cup uncooked Minute Rice
   (Cooks to about 3 cups)
2 eggs, beaten
$^1/_2$ pound Velveeta cheese,
   grated

1 medium onion, chopped
2 tablespoons parsley
$^1/_2$ cup Wesson Oil
1 teaspoon red pepper
   Salt to taste

Cook the rice as directed, add the beaten eggs and other ingredients and bake in a greased casserole at 350 degrees, covered for the first 30 minutes, and remove the cover for the last 15 minutes of cooking time. The teaspoon of red pepper is the secret ingredient. Your taste may require more or less.

Ethel Morehead, Plainview

SPOON BREAD

To one cup of water add 1 teaspoon of shortening, 1 tablespoon of sugar and $^2/_3$ teaspoon of salt. Let this come to a boil, remove from stove and immediately add one cup of corn meal, stirring in a bit at a time. Cool slightly. Beat two eggs, add one cup of sweet milk and stir this into the meal mixture, beating thoroughly.

Have 1 tablespoon of shortening in baking dish, heating in the oven. Add 1 teaspoon baking powder to bread mixture and pour into baking dish, which should be very hot. Cook for 45 minutes at 375 degrees.

SIDE DISHES

(Mrs. Cape shares the above 17th century recipe with us that comes by way of her family from the kitchen of Frances Jones Dendridge, the mother of Martha Washington. Mrs. Cape considers it fool-proof and has never had a serving left over. Try it with venison roast.)

Clara Louise Cape, San Marcos

JANEY'S FLOUR TORTILLA RECIPE

1 cup flour
2 teaspoons baking powder

$^1/_2$ teaspoon salt
2 tablespoons Crisco

Blend with pastry fork as you would for pie crust. Add about $^1/_4$ cup (more or less) water. Work the dough until it is smooth and satiny. Form into ball. Turn bowl over on top and let it rest for $^1/_2$ hour, then pinch out individual tortillas about the size of a walnut. Roll round and flatten. Cook in ungreased skillet to brown on both sides.

Janey Briscoe, Uvalde

CORNBREAD

This basic recipe was given by a Negro woman (name unknown) at the grocery store the first year of our marriage. This recipe may be doubled or tripled depending on your crowd. The one cup basic makes about six muffins or a small tin of corn bread.

$^3/_4$ cup of yellow corn meal
$^1/_4$ cup of flour
2 teaspoons baking powder
$^1/_2$ teaspoon salt
$^1/_2$ teaspoon sugar

1 egg, slightly beaten
$^3/_4$ cup of buttermilk to which
$^1/_4$ teaspoon of baking
    soda has been added or
$^3/_4$ cup of sweet milk

Mix all together and pour into heated muffin pans or skillet to which 2 tablespoons of cooking oil or shortening has been added. Bake at 425 degrees for 25 minutes.

This may be spiced up by the addition of canned corn, pimientos and jalapeno peppers.

Easier still, buy the packaged mix at the grocery store.

BROCCOLI RICE CASSEROLE

1 cup of chopped onion
1 cup of chopped celery
2 tablespoons oil
1 can of cream of chicken soup
1 small can of evaporated milk

2 cups of cooked rice
1 package chopped broccoli —
   thawed
1 can of sliced water chestnuts

Sauté onions and celery in oil until soft. Combine with remaining ingredients in greased 2-quart casserole. Cover and bake at 350 degrees for 40 minutes. Yield: 8–10 servings.

Ethel Cone

PEPPER JELLY

1 cup of jalapeno peppers,
   chopped fine
6 cups sugar

1½ cup of white vinegar
1 bottle Certo

Cook the first three ingredients until mixture comes to a full boil. Turn down heat and boil for 5 minutes. Remove from heat and add Certo. Strain and pour into hot sterilized jars and seal.

Ethel Cone

WILD PLUM JELLY

A tart jelly adds greatly to any game meal and the very best is WILD PLUM. There are many varieties of wild plum in Texas but the one we have access to is a small, very tart, deep red one that ripens in the fall.

5 pounds of wild plums (stemmed and washed)
7½ cups sugar or 3¼ pounds
1 package of SURE JELL

Place the 5 pounds of washed plums in a very large jelly kettle and cover with water. Simmer gently until the plums have burst. You may stir and mash them to help the process along.

Strain the juice through cheese cloth. You will need 5 cups of juice, so if not enough juice is present after straining pour enough hot water through the cheese cloth to make up the desired volume.

Heat the juice with the SURE JELL until it is boiling. Add

SIDE DISHES

77

all of the sugar at once and stir constantly. When the mixture has come to a full, rolling boil that cannot be stirred down, boil for one minute and remove from the heat.

Skim and ladle into hot, sterilized jars and seal at once with paraffin or sterilized lids. This should make 8−12 six ounce jars.

Many jelly makers maintain that there is plenty of pectin in wild plums to make jelly without the use of SURE JELL. I have tried it both ways and find you get a better yield and a more uniform product with the addition of pectin.

HOMINY CASSEROLE

1 medium onion, chopped
1 green pepper, chopped
1 large can of hominy, well drained
2 fresh tomatoes, peeled and cut up

$^1/_2$ can (small) of green chili peppers, chopped (NOT hot)
Salt and pepper to taste

Mix all together and place in greased casserole. Bake 30 minutes at 325 degrees. Grate cheddar cheese over the top and return to the oven long enough for the cheese to melt.

Gladys Robinson, Plainview

FRIED ONION RINGS

We discovered this recipe accidentally, while preparing a makeshift supper at our ranch camphouse. A sack of oversized white onions had been "gifted" us at the packing shed in Floydada, too large to market in grocery stores (that's the truth).

We sliced these kingsized onions, then soaked them in ice water until crisp. Next we dipped the rings in a batter of slightly beaten whole egg and packaged pancake mix (this was a man's idea). Fried in deep fat, the onions came out tender, sweet, altogether delicious and nutritious. Try this as an addition to any game dinner — or even as an hors d'oeuvre.

Incidentally, onions can be sliced and frozen for future use.

SIDE DISHES

RED SALADS TO ACCOMPANY GAME DINNERS

Cranberries and cherries give the added color and tartness desirable for a wild game dinner.

CRANBERRY SALAD

1 package raspberry gelatin
1¼ cups of hot water
1 1-pound can of whole
    cranberry sauce

1 cup of commercial sour
    cream
½ cup of chopped nuts

Dissolve gelatin in hot water and chill until slightly thickened. Fold in remaining ingredients. Pour into individual molds or one large one. Chill until set and serve on salad greens. Serves six to eight.

Mary Menon English, Dallas

For those who find the gelatin too sweet for your taste, try this adaption from Margery McKee, Austin:

¼ cup of water
1½ packages of unflavored
    gelatin
1¼ cups of hot cranberry juice
    cocktail
1 1-pound can of whole
    cranberry sauce

1 cup of commercial sour
    cream
½ cup of chopped nuts
½ cup of finely chopped
    celery

JEWEL SALAD

1 package of raspberry gelatin
1 cup hot water
½ cup of cold water

2 cups of fresh cranberries
1 whole orange
1 cup sugar

Dissolve the gelatin in hot water and set aside to chill.

Quarter the unpeeled orange and run it through the food chopper followed by the two cups of washed cranberries. Save the juice. Add sugar to the ground mixture and stir until dissolved. Add the fruit and berries to the chilled gelatin mixture and mold as desired.

SIDE DISHES

GINGER CRANBERRIES

4 cups (1 pound) fresh
   cranberries
1 large orange, quartered
1 cup raisins

$^1/_2$ cup honey
$^3/_4$ cup sugar
$1^1/_2$ teaspoon powdered ginger

Put all ingredients through the food chopper — mix with sugar, honey and ginger. Chill to mold.

CHERRY — BURGUNDY SALAD

1 package of black cherry
   gelatin
1 can pitted Bing cherries
$1^1/_2$ cups of burgundy wine

1 small bottle of stuffed green
   olives
$^1/_4$ cup of chopped celery

Dissolve gelatin in one-half cup of hot water. Add $1^1/_2$ cups of wine and chill until slightly thickened. Add cherries which have been thoroughly drained, olives, drained and chopped celery. Place in individual molds to serve on lettuce. Top at serving time with mayonnaise, sour cream or yogurt.

Lucile H. English, Plainview

BARBECUE SALAD ASPIC

1 package lemon gelatin
$1^1/_4$ cups of hot water or less
1 8 ounce can tomato sauce
$1^1/_2$ tablespoons vinegar or
   lemon juice
$^1/_2$ teaspoon salt
Dash of pepper

Add as you wish:
onion juice
Worcestershire (a few drops)
horseradish
cayenne
garlic and/or celery salt

Dissolve gelatin, cool and add the other ingredients. Chill until firm.

This is beautiful and tasty served on a slice of tomato with avocado, asparagus and hard-boiled egg.

Margaret G. Battle, Austin

PINTO BEANS

Pinto beans, essential to any good barbecue meal, can be cooked about as many ways as there are cooks. Usually, the pinto bean expert is as convinced that his way is best as a hound dog man betting his pet leads the pack.

Former Governor Coke Stevenson ranks among the all-time champion bean chefs. He learned as a pioneer teamster hauling supplies across the hill country, and practiced the art through a long life as lawyer and public official.

"Governor Coke" washed and picked his beans, then started cooking immediately in a pot of boiling water. The boiling water keeps the bean skin firm while the inside becomes tender and soft. He omits salt and fat meat from beans.

. . . Our longtime family cook, Alberta Walker, washed and picked beans, then soaked them overnight in cold water. The beans are started to cook in the soak water to which a pinch of soda is added.

Soaked beans require less time to cook, and the skin becomes softer. Alberta added: salt, a tablespoon of sugar and one-fourth to one-half pound of salt pork or several tablespoonfuls of bacon drippings (for every pound of dried beans used).

Mrs. Lucile H. English, Judy's mother, cooked chili beans in winter on the Texas plains. After soaking the beans overnight, she cooked them slowly, adding salt, sugar, ground or fat meat, canned tomatoes, and several tablespoons of chili powder as the cooking progressed.

With cornbread, fruit or green salad, this makes a very filling meal.

CHOW-CHOW

Chow-Chow is a green tomato relish made by Judy's mother and grandmother at the end of the summer just before frost nipped the last vegetables in the garden. Grandmother gathered the tomatoes, green peppers (and those that had turned red on

SIDE DISHES

the vine) plus onions, small cucumbers, and even the small un-ripened melons that were left on the vine. There are many variations on this theme but the crisp, tart relish is very closely associated in memory with the duck season on the high plains and the first frost which is "hog-killing" time.

Chow-Chow is especially good served with wild duck and goose.

For every gallon of chopped vegetables add:

2 cups of sugar	2 tablespoons of prepared
2 cups of water	mustard
2 cups of vinegar	1 teaspoon each of pepper,
2 tablespoons of salt	cloves and allspice

Use twice as many cups of chopped green tomatoes as the other vegetables. Include onion and green peppers, but one may also include cabbage, carrots, cauliflower, or any other vegetables you wish to pickle.

Pour boiling water over chopped vegetables. Let blanch for a few minutes.

Drain and add all of the pickling ingredients.

Boil for 15–20 minutes.

Put in sterilized jars and seal hot.

BEAN SALAD

For the Fourth of July picnic when cool beans are substituted for pintos, this salad can be made the day before and stored in a glass container until serving time.

1 can yellow wax beans
1 can French cut green beans
1 can red kidney beans
1 can garbanzos
½ cup cider vinegar
½ cup salad oil

½ cup grated onion
½ cup of chopped green
   pepper
1 teaspoon salt
1 teaspoon pepper

Cover and chill at least eight hours before serving.

Marjorie Overly, California

KRAUT RELISH

This relish is a great addition to any game dinner. It keeps almost indefinitely, when refrigerated. Americans who have resided in the Orient, particularly military men, may be less enthusiastic about this dish which reminds them of an aromatic Far Eastern concoction called Kim Chee.

1 pound drained sauerkraut
¾ cup sugar
½ green pepper, chopped

2 ribs of celery, chopped
2 small onions, chopped
1 teaspoon tumeric

Mix together in a glass dish. Cover with cider vinegar. Let stand 24 hours before serving.

Mrs. J.N.R. Score